Marian Devotions
in the Domestic Church

Marian Devotions in the Domestic Church

CATHERINE AND PETER FOURNIER

IGNATIUS PRESS   SAN FRANCISCO

Dedication

For our Mother—and our mothers.

Mothers are both the initiators and the custodians of culture. Mothers teach, defend, and preserve culture—the sum of those beliefs, stories, traditions, practices, recipes, and customs that express the identity and shared values of a family, a neighborhood, a nation, an ethnic group, or a Faith.

Our Blessed Mother, our "Mother most amiable", is at once both the initiator and the custodian of Catholic culture. In her numerous apparitions and in our devotional activities honoring her, the Virgin Mary teaches and defends, transmits and preserves our identity as her children and as the beloved children of God.

Scripture quotations are from the Holy Bible, Revised Standard Version, Catholic Edition. The Old Testament, © 1952; the Apocrypha, © 1957; the New Testament, © 1946; the Catholic Edition of the Old Testament, incorporating the Apocrypha, © 1966; the Catholic Edition of the New Testament, © 1966 by the Division of Christian Education of the National Council of the Churches of Christ in the United States of America.

Excerpts from the English translation of the *Catechism of the Catholic Church* for use in the United States of America copyright © 1994, United States Catholic Conference, Inc.—Libreria Editrice Vaticana. English translation of the *Catechism of the Catholic Church: Modifications from the Editio Typica* copyright © 1997, United States Catholic Conference, Inc.—Libreria Editrice Vaticana. Used with permission.

Book design by Peter and Catherine Fournier.
Articles written and illustrated by Catherine Fournier.
The Mysteries of the Rosary and the coloring-page art on pages 81–90 are by Jennifer DeFillipo.

Published in 2007 by Ignatius Press, San Francisco.

ISBN: 978-1-58617-074-5
Library of Congress Control Number 2004114956

Printed in the United States of America ∞

Contents

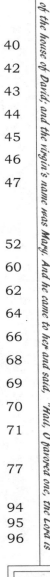

of the house of David; and the virgin's name was Mary. And he came to her and said, "Hail, O favored one, the Lord is

And the angel said to her, "Do not be afraid, Mary, for you have found favor with God. And behold, you will conceive in your womb and bear a son, and you shall call his

with you!" But she was greatly troubled at the saying, and considered in her mind what sort of greeting this might be.

A Place in All Seasons

In 1974, Pope Paul VI published an apostolic exhortation titled *Marialis Cultus* (For the Right Ordering and Development of Devotion to the Blessed Virgin Mary). In it, he examined and answered a growing tendency in the Church to regard devotion to Mary as a distraction and hindrance to developing a love for our Lord.

Pope Paul VI assured us that Mary leads us to her Son and that she has demonstrated for us an example of faithful obedience to God. He said, "Mary is not only an example for the whole Church in the exercise of divine worship but is also, clearly, a teacher of the spiritual life for individual Christians." (See the *Catechism of the Catholic Church* [hereafter CCC] no. 2030.)

Pope Paul VI recommended the feasts of Mary that "include the commemoration of Christ's Mother in the annual cycle of the mysteries of her Son".

Among the Marian feasts recommended by Paul VI, along with several others of importance, are the following:

January 1:	Solemnity of Mary, Mother of God
February 2:	Feast of the Presentation of the Lord
February 11:	Our Lady of Lourdes
March 25:	Solemnity of the Annunciation
May 24:	Mary, Help of Christians
May 31:	Feast of the Visitation
June 27:	Our Lady of Perpetual Help
July 16:	Our Lady of Mount Carmel
August 5:	Dedication of Saint Mary Major
August 15:	Solemnity of the Assumption
August 22:	Memorial of the Queenship of Mary
September 8:	Feast of the Birth of Mary
September 15:	Memorial of Our Lady of Sorrows
October 7:	Memorial of Our Lady of the Rosary
November 21:	Memorial of the Presentation of Mary
December 8:	Solemnity of the Immaculate Conception
December 12:	Feast of Our Lady of Guadalupe
December 25:	Solemnity of Christmas

Paul VI also recommended the Optional Memorial of the Immaculate Heart of Mary, and Saturday Masses of our Lady.

The CCC (no. 971) quotes Pope Paul VI's words: "'The Church's devotion to the Blessed Virgin is intrinsic to Christian worship' (Lk 1:48; Paul VI, *MC* 56). The Church rightly honors the 'Blessed Virgin with special devotion. From the most ancient times the Blessed Virgin has been honored with the title of "Mother of God", to whose protection the faithful fly in all their dangers and needs. . . . This very special devotion . . . differs essentially from the adoration which is given to the incarnate Word and equally to the Father and the Holy Spirit, and greatly fosters this adoration' (*LG* 66). The liturgical feasts dedicated to the Mother of God and Marian prayer, such as the rosary, an 'epitome of the whole Gospel', express this devotion to the Virgin Mary (cf. Paul VI, *MC* 42; *SC* 103)."

Marian devotions find a place in all seasons and all stages of life. As part of family life, they help the family and its individual members grow in their spiritual lives as they learn from Mary's example and follow her guiding hand to her Son. (See CCC nos. 1655–57.)

This book suggests many ways to incorporate a devotion to Mary into your domestic church, through family activities, prayers, observance of many of the feasts recommended by Pope Paul VI, crafts, and coloring pictures. Each Marian feast, approximately one for each month of the year, is presented here with a brief outline, some history, and suggestions for celebration. There are literally hundreds of feasts honoring our Lady.

May our Lady bless your home and family!

Catherine Fournier

Note: For additional copies of the coloring pictures and craft patterns, visit our "secret" web page at http://www.domestic-church.com/index.dir/index_ref_mary.htm/.

Family Activities

overshadow you; therefore the child to be born will be called holy, the Son of God. And behold, your kinswoman Elizabeth in her old age has also conceived a son; and this is the

Family Consecration

Consecration

"The solemn blessing dedicating a person, a place or a thing to the service of God"—*Concise Catholic Dictionary*, compiled by Robert C. Broderick, M.A. (St. Paul. Minn.: Catechetical Guild Society, 1944).

In his letter to families entitled *Familiaris Consortio*, Pope John Paul II describes the incredible potential and divine mystery of each family created through the sacrament of marriage. Families, he says, are "the cradle and the setting" of the Church. The people of the Church spring from the family, and the family is the recipient of the spiritual nurturing, protection, and teaching of the Church.

The Pope tells families that in their foundation and action they are dedicated to creating, nurturing, and benefiting the community of saints and the greater glory of God. We do not marry or have children for our own purposes; we enter into marriage as our vocation, our way of serving God in our lives. We commit to serving God through our families and helping each other achieve heaven. (See CCC no. 1601.)

A family consecration brings this (perhaps unspoken) desire to life. As the definition above explains, it solemnly blesses and dedicates the members of the family to the service of God, expressing their love, trust, and faith in His protection. It should not be taken lightly. Careful consideration, discussion, and explanation (especially to the younger members of the family) are important.

Like the consecration of a building or the Consecration at Mass, a family consecration requires preparation, both spiritual and physical.

"Prayer is the raising of one's mind and heart to God or the requesting of good things from God" (CCC no. 2559, quoting St. John Damascene, *De fide orth.* 3, 24: PG 94, 1089C). Our prayers are songs of praise, statements of intent, and requests for assistance. And because we are fallible and sinful, we need to pray often to refresh and renew our desire and determination to follow God.

For this reason, while a family consecration could be a single event in the life of the family, it is best repeated yearly. As the children of the family grow, their understanding of this prayer and devotion will mature and deepen.

There are many prayers of consecration that can help to consecrate the family to the Sacred Heart of Jesus, to the Immaculate Heart of Mary, or to the Holy Family. A few of the many possibilities follow.

Preparations

Plan to make the consecration on a special day, preferably on a feast day (of our Lady if you are making a consecration to Mary), though the anniversary of your wedding or your entrance into the Church if you are a convert would also be appropriate. Discuss the meaning and importance of your family consecration and the day you have chosen with your children. Since a consecration is a statement of intent, they should not be passive participants. Encourage them to ask questions, make suggestions, and add their special petitions and intentions to those of the family.

As a family, make a small act of penance on the day of the consecration. This can be whatever you wish according to the abilities and capacities of the family: a fast; an alms offering; the lighting of a candle; making a pilgrimage to a Marian shrine; or some other action in honor of our Lady, her Son, or our Heavenly Father. If at all possible, go to confession and attend Mass on this day as well.

Be sure to place some remembrance of your family consecration in your home. Consider hanging an icon or other holy picture over your family altar or placing a statue on the altar or somewhere else in the home.

Acts of Consecration

Prayer of Total Consecration

O Immaculata, queen of heaven and earth, refuge of sinners and our most loving Mother, God has willed to entrust the entire order of mercy to you. I, [name], a repentant sinner, cast myself at your feet, humbly imploring you to take me with all that I am and have, wholly to yourself as your possession and property.

Please make of me, of all my powers of soul and body, of my whole life, death and eternity, whatever most pleases you.

If it pleases you, use all that I am and have without reserve, wholly to accomplish what was said of you:

"She will crush your head", and "You alone have destroyed all heresies in the whole world." Let me be a fit instrument in your immaculate and merciful hands for introducing and increasing your glory to the maximum in all the many strayed and indifferent souls and thus help extend as far as possible the blessed kingdom of the most Sacred Heart of Jesus. For wherever you enter you obtain the grace of conversion and growth in holiness, since it is through your hands that all graces come to us from the most Sacred Heart of Jesus.

V. Allow me to praise you, O Sacred Virgin.
R. Give me strength against your enemies.

Daily Consecration to Mary

Queen of the Most Holy Rosary, I renew my consecration to you and to your Immaculate Heart. Please accept me, my dear Mother, and use me as you wish to accomplish your designs upon the world. I am all yours, my Mother, my Queen, and all that I have is yours.

A Child's Consecration to Mary

Dear Mary, my holy Mother, I love you so much, and I give you my heart. Help me to love God. Help me to love my neighbor as a child of God. Help me to love myself as a child of God. Amen.

Act of Consecration to the Immaculate Heart of Mary

I, [name], a faithless sinner, renew and ratify today in thy hands, O Immaculate Mother, the vows of my baptism; I renounce forever Satan, his pomps and works; and give myself entirely to Jesus Christ, the Incarnate Wisdom, to carry my cross after Him all the days of my life, and to be more faithful to Him than I have ever been before.

In the presence of all the heavenly court I choose thee this day, for my Mother. I deliver and consecrate to thee, as thy slave, my body and soul, my goods, both interior and exterior, and even the value of all my good actions, past, present, and future; leaving to thee the entire and full right of disposing of me, and all that belongs to me, without exception, according to thy good pleasure, for the greater glory of God, in time and in eternity. Amen.

Prayer for the Consecration of the Family

Most Sacred Hearts of Jesus and Mary, I consecrate myself and my whole family to you. We consecrate to you our very being and all our life; all that we are, all that we have, and all that we love. To you we give our bodies, our hearts, and our souls. To you we dedicate our home and our country.

Mindful of this consecration, we now promise you to live the Christian way by the practice of Christian virtues, without regard for human respect. O most Sacred Hearts of Jesus and Mary, accept our humble confidence and this act of consecration by which we entrust ourselves and all our family to you. In you, we put all our hope, and we shall never be confounded.

Most Sacred Heart of Jesus, have mercy on us.
Immaculate Heart of Mary, be our salvation. Amen.

Family Consecration to the Sacred Heart of Jesus

O most Sacred Heart of Jesus, we come to You as a family and consecrate ourselves to Your Sacred Heart. Protect us through Your Most Precious Blood, and keep us pure and holy.

O Dear Jesus, we are so far away from Your most pure and Sacred Heart.

As a family we need Your help. Heal all the quarrels that exist in our family due to our unforgivingness and lack of love for You. Heal our unbelieving and unconverted hearts and lead us to Your Sacred Heart with love. Unite us as a family and remove all stain of sinfulness from our souls. Help us to be a prayerful and loving family, so that through our example we may lead other souls to Your Most Sacred Heart.

We give You our hearts, dearest Jesus, and consecrate our family through the fourth generation. Through the prayers of our dearest Mother Mary, may we live this consecration every day of our lives. Amen.

Most Sacred Heart of Jesus, have pity on us.

—Origin unknown (contributed by Mary Stelley)

Family Consecration to the Immaculate Heart of Mary

O Mother most pure, we come to you as a family and consecrate ourselves to your most Immaculate Heart. We come to you as a family and place our trust in your powerful intercession.

O dearest Mother Mary, teach us as a mother teaches her children, for our souls are soiled and our prayers are weak because of our sinful hearts. Here we are, dearest Mother, ready to respond to you and follow your way, for your way leads us to the heart of your Son, Jesus. We are ready to be cleansed and purified.

Come then, Virgin Most Pure, and embrace us with your motherly mantle. Make our hearts whiter than snow and as pure as a spring of fresh water.

Teach us to pray, so that our prayers may become more beautiful than the singing of the birds at the break of dawn.

Dear Mother Mary, we entrust to your Immaculate Heart of Hearts our family and our entire future. Lead us all to our homeland, which is heaven. Amen.

Immaculate Heart of Mary, pray for us.

—Origin unknown (contributed by Mary Stelley)

MARY'S FLOWERS

Marigold   Both the English marigold "calendula" and the French or garden marigold were used as gold-colored dye for wool. Marigolds symbolize Mary's domesticity and also sometimes her sorrows, as the the blossom's strong scent reminded people of burial ointments.

Violet   The small, delicate violet, with its faint, sweet fragrance and heart-shaped leaves, reminds us of Mary—her humility, purity, and faithfulness.

The Angelus and the Regina Caeli

From Old Testament times, it has been customary for observant Jews to pray three times a day: in the morning, at three o'clock in the afternoon, and at night. (Read Daniel 6:10 for an example of this practice.) The Apostles maintained this tradition, as we can read in the Acts of the Apostles (3:1) of Peter and John going to the temple "at the ninth hour of prayer".

The Angelus devotion, honoring the Incarnation, follows the habit of praying three times daily, at six o'clock in the morning, noon, and six o'clock in the evening. In many places around the world, church bells ring at those same times, to call the faithful to pray the Angelus.

For us too, the Angelus provides families an opportunity to gather together before everyone's day begins, to take a moment in the middle of the day to ask Mary's intercession in our lives, and to come together at the end of the day to give thanks to God for all the blessings of the day. (See CCC nos. 2660, 2676-77, 2694.) The words of the Angelus echo the Gospel of Luke at the Annunciation and Incarnation.

During the year, outside the Easter season:

THE ANGELUS

Leader: The angel of the Lord declared unto Mary.

Response: And she conceived by the Holy Spirit.

Leader: Hail, Mary, full of grace,
the Lord is with thee.
Blessed art thou among women,
and blessed is the fruit of thy womb, Jesus.

Response: Holy Mary, Mother of God,
pray for us sinners
now and at the hour of our death. Amen.

Leader: Behold the handmaid of the Lord.

Response: Be it done unto me according to thy word.

Repeat the Hail Mary.

Leader: And the Word was made Flesh.

Response: And dwelt among us.

Repeat the Hail Mary.

Leader: Pray for us, O Holy Mother of God.

Response: That we may be made worthy of the promises of Christ.

Leader: Pour forth, we beg You, O Lord, Your grace into our hearts, that we, to whom the Incarnation of Christ Your Son was made known by the message of an angel, may by His Passion and Cross be brought to the glory of His Resurrection. Through the same Christ our Lord.

All: Amen.

During the Easter season:

REGINA CAELI

All: Queen of heaven, rejoice, Alleluia,

For He whom you merited to bear, Alleluia,

Has risen, as He said, Alleluia.

Pray for us to God, Alleluia.

Leader: Rejoice and be glad, O Virgin Mary, Alleluia.

Response: Because the Lord is truly risen, Alleluia.

Leader: Let us pray. O God, who by the Resurrection of Your Son, our Lord Jesus Christ, gave joy to the whole world; grant, we beg You, that through the intercession of the Virgin Mary, His Mother, we may lay hold of the joys of eternal life. Through the same Christ our Lord.

All: Amen.

his handmaiden. For behold, henceforth all generations will call me blessed; for he who is mighty has done great things for me, and holy is his name. And his mercy is on those who

The Rosary

Mary said, "My soul magnifies the Lord, and my spirit rejoices in God my Savior, for he has regarded the low estate of

The Origin of the Rosary

Like many other traditions and prayers of our Catholic Faith—for example, praying the Our Father or celebrating the feast of the Nativity—the Rosary is so much a part of the practice of our Faith that it is hard to imagine a time without this prayer. Yet, almost one thousand years of Church history passed before the early versions (and variations) of the Rosary appeared.

At first, the laity developed a practice of saying 150 Our Fathers in response to the daily reading of the 150 Psalms by local monks. This practice, called the "Psalter", was encouraged by the Church and enhanced by the addition of meditations for each prayer. (See CCC nos. 2678–79.)

Gradually, the prayers were arranged into three groups of fifty. Then, an early (short) version of the Hail Mary and the Apostles' Creed were added to the prayers, and a series of meditations were associated with groups of ten prayers. Eventually, an arrangement that used 150 Hail Marys was developed and became known as "Mary's Psalter".

In the early 1200s, the Albigensian heresy took hold in France and other parts of Europe. The Albigensians believed that there was no heaven, no hell, and no moral code, and therefore that adultery, fornication, and suicide were acceptable activities. Saint Dominic and other Catholic priests preached against this heresy, but were not altogether successful.

According to Blessed Alan de la Roche, who wrote an account about 250 years later, our Lady appeared to Saint Dominic and said: "I want you to know that, in this kind of warfare, the battering ram has always been the Angelic Psalter, which is the foundation stone of the New Testament. Therefore, if you want to reach these hardened souls and win them over to God, preach my Psalter."

Saint Dominic began to teach and preach about the Rosary and its lessons. Within months, most of France had returned to Catholicism.

The Rosary: A Gift for Our Day

—by Monsignor Thomas Wells (1944–2000)

"October is the month of the Holy Rosary, the month when the Church reminds us of the value of this beautiful method of prayer. I know that I find the Rosary an ever greater gift in my life: not because I pray so well, but because I pray so poorly. Some historians speculate that the origins of the Rosary go back to efforts, even before the Middle Ages, to help illiterate lay brothers in monasteries and laity in the fields to pray.

"The monks could pray the psalms and read the Gospels and, in them, find fruit for prayer, but those who could not read had little for spiritual inspiration. (Incidentally, stained glass windows in the great cathedrals served the same purpose. They could be 'read' by the illiterate in such a way that the truths were taught to those who could not read.) At first, apparently, the people were encouraged to pray, for example, one hundred and fifty Our Fathers. (The Hail Mary, as we know it today, was not known before about the twelfth century.)

"The repetition of prayers, which we sometimes find difficult, is a practice known throughout world religions. This repetition can free the mind from having to find things to say to God and allow the person to hear what God might be saying. Beads strung together to help in the counting of prayers is also a very ancient practice. The development of the decades of ten Hail Marys separated by the Our Father and the meditation on particular mysteries of the life of Christ and our Lady gradually came about as more effort was given to teaching the laity to pray.

"The Rosary is such a gift for our day because, while we have the ability to read and thus use Scripture or other spiritual aids in trying to pray, many feel they have not the time. The Rosary solves the problem. I know people who pray the Rosary on the subway, who say it while commuting or while going through the torture of running for exercise. Probably they will never become mystics in their prayer, but at least they give time to the Lord

each day and ask the prayers of His Mother on behalf of themselves and those they love.

"No matter when we say it, whether alone or with others, whether in the quiet of the evening or in the chaos of the highway, let us use this month of the Rosary to join countless millions who have gone before us in this prayer with our Lady to the Glory of God."

The Family Devotion of the Rosary

The Rosary has been called the most beautiful and powerful of all the Church's devotions. It appeals to everyone: the old and the young, the clergy and the laity. The Rosary helps bring the lukewarm or fallen-away back to the Church and strengthens the faithful in their spiritual lives. (See CCC no. 971.)

With this history and its power, the Rosary is also possibly the most idealized of devotions, the one that most parents aspire to for their families to pray, the one they chide themselves about. We gaze around our living rooms, at the somnolent or sullen teens; at the eight- and ten-year-olds, locked in a silly-face contest; and at the toddler, squirming half on and half off the couch—and wonder why we can't pray the Rosary properly "like other families".

Well, take heart. You *are* praying the Rosary like other families. We all struggle to achieve peace, harmony, and attention while praying the family Rosary. Family prayer improves with time and practice. It can become one of the joys of family life, with prayer

time being a relaxed and happy time for your family. (See CCC nos. 2660, 2694.)

There are a few steps parents can take to improve their family's practice of this devotion:

Be persistent: Don't get discouraged; keep trying. Find a time or place that works for your family and stick to it.

Be prudent: Be reasonable about your family's capacity. Don't overload them.

Be flexible: Be creative about where and when to pray the Rosary. Try to pray in the car, or a single decade as part of evening prayers, or a five-decade Rosary first thing in the morning.

How To Pray the Rosary

"Saying" a Rosary means reciting five or six prayers, four of them repeatedly, while meditating on the events in the life of Mary and Jesus.

First, make the Sign of the Cross. With the help of rosary beads, begin at the crucifix and pray the *Apostles' Creed*.

At the first large bead next to the crucifix, say the *Our Father*. At the next three, smaller beads, say three *Hail Marys*. At the following large bead, say a *Glory Be*, announce the mystery to be meditated, and pray an *Our Father*.

Follow the same pattern for the remainder of the Rosary, ending each group of ten beads (a decade) with a *Glory Be*, a statement of the meditation theme, and pray an *Our Father*.

When you have finished praying five decades (once around the rosary) or fifteen decades (three times around the rosary), end with the *Hail, Holy Queen*.

Saint Louis de Montfort, a Dominican priest with a great devotion to Mary, added the *Glory Be* to the prayers of our Rosary. It is now customary also to add the *O My Jesus* prayer after each *Glory Be*, as requested by Our Lady of Fatima.

The Joyful Mysteries

First Joyful Mystery
The Annunciation
Luke 1:26-38

The whole world was waiting for the Messiah. God promised to send His people a Savior. He would be a King, said the prophecies. He would open the way to heaven, which was closed when Adam and Eve disobeyed God.

Still, Mary of Nazareth was surprised when the Angel Gabriel appeared to her, saying, "Hail, full of grace." The angel told her she had been chosen as Mother of God. "How can this be?" she asked and then said, "Let it be done according to Your will." In that instant, Jesus was conceived through the power of the Holy Spirit and became man. What joy, thanks to the trust and humility of Mary!

Let this mystery teach us to be humble.

Second Joyful Mystery
The Visitation
Luke 1:39-56

The Angel Gabriel told Mary that her cousin Elizabeth was going to have a baby son. This was joyful news. Elizabeth and her husband, Zechariah, were very old. They had no children to care for them in their old age. Mary went to help Elizabeth with her pregnancy.

When Mary arrived at Elizabeth's house, Elizabeth called out, "Who am I that the Mother of my Lord should come to me? Blessed are thou among women and blessed is the fruit of thy womb!" Mary replied with a song of praise called a "Canticle". Mary took care of Elizabeth until the baby, John, was born. What joy for us all, thanks to the love and charity of Mary!

Let this mystery teach us to be charitable.

Third Joyful Mystery
The Nativity
Luke 2:1-7

The Roman emperor ordered a census of all the land. Joseph and Mary left Nazareth and traveled to Bethlehem to answer the census. When they arrived, Bethlehem was very crowded. Mary and Joseph wondered what they should do. They were poor, and the inns were all full. The baby was coming soon, and they had nowhere to stay.

But they did not worry. They knew God was watching over them. So Mary's son, Jesus, the Son of God and the Savior of the world, was born in a stable with God's creatures around Him. What joy for us all, that God watches over us the way He watched over the Holy Family that night!

Let this mystery teach us to trust God in all things.

Fourth Joyful Mystery
The Presentation
Luke 2:22-38

Jewish law says that a first-born son must be presented to God in thanks for His great works. Mary and Joseph obeyed this law. They took Jesus to the temple in Jerusalem when He was forty days old. They offered a sacrifice and gave thanks to God.

An old man named Simeon waited his whole life to see the Messiah. He recognized the child as the promised Savior and praised God. He also made a prophecy about Jesus' ministry, telling Mary that she would have great joy and great sadness. An old woman named Anna also saw that Jesus was the Messiah and gave thanks to God for His answer to the Jewish people's prayers. What joy for all of us in the marvelous works of God!

Let this mystery teach us to give thanks to God for His great works.

Fifth Joyful Mystery
The Finding in the Temple
Luke 2:41-52

When Jesus was twelve, the Holy Family traveled to Jerusalem for the great Passover feast. They went with many other pilgrims from Nazareth. On the way home, Mary and Joseph did not see Jesus in the group. They thought He was walking with friends. But Jesus was left behind in Jerusalem!

Mary and Joseph searched for Jesus for three whole days. They were very worried. Finally, they found Him in the great temple, talking to the priests. The priests were amazed at His understanding of God's teachings. Mary and Joseph were just glad to find Him. They asked why He had left them. Jesus answered, "Do you not understand I must do My Father's work?" He obeyed His parents and returned to Nazareth with them. What joy for all of us in obeying our parents, because it is obeying God too!

Let this mystery teach us how to live in obedience.

The Franciscan Crown

This devotion is also known as the Rosary of the Seven Joys of Mary.

These seven joys are:

The Annunciation

The Visitation

The Birth of Our Lord

The Adoration of the Magi

The Finding of the Child Jesus in the Temple

The Resurrection of Our Lord

The Assumption of the Blessed Virgin and Her Coronation in Heaven

Used by the members of the three orders of Saint Francis, the Franciscan Crown begins with the Apostles' Creed, the Our Father, and three Hail Marys as usual, and then consists of *seven* decades made up of one Our Father and ten Hail Marys.

The Joys of Mary are introduced after the word "Jesus" in the first Hail Mary of the decade. For example: ". . . the fruit of thy womb, Jesus, *whom you joyfully conceived*".

At the end of the seventh decade, two extra Hail Marys are added to make a total of 72—the apocryphal age of the Blessed Virgin at the time of her Assumption. The Franciscan Crown then concludes with the usual Hail, Holy Queen.

The Sorrowful Mysteries

First Sorrowful Mystery
The Agony in the Garden
Matthew 26:36-39, Mark 14:32-36

Jesus celebrated the Passover feast with His disciples. He gave them the Eucharist at His Last Supper. Then Jesus went to the garden of Gethsemane to pray. He knew that His time on earth was almost finished. He also knew that the next day would be very hard. He was going to die for our sins.

Jesus prayed, "Father, let these things not happen, if it is Your will. But I want to do Your will, not Mine." An angel came to Him and comforted Him as he prayed. Jesus was like us in all things but sin, yet He died to save us from sin. What great sorrow for all of us that the innocent victim died for our sins!

Let this mystery teach us to be truly sorry for our sins.

Second Sorrowful Mystery
The Scourging
Mark 15:15, John 19:1

Soldiers came to arrest Jesus and to take Him to stand before the high priests. The priests questioned Him about being the Son of God. They were angry and said He was lying. They wanted Jesus to stop teaching the people about God the Father. So, they told the soldiers to take Jesus to Pontius Pilate's palace.

There, the soldiers took off Jesus' clothes and tied him to a pillar. They beat Him with a whip. They hurt Him to make Him say He was not the Son of God. But Jesus wanted to do His Father's will even when it was hard, so He stayed silent. What great sorrow for all of us that Jesus was punished for our sins!

Let this mystery teach us to accept God's will.

Third Sorrowful Mystery
The Crowning with Thorns
Matthew 27:29-31, Mark 15:16-20, John 19:2-3

After Jesus was beaten, the soldiers laughed at Him. "You call yourself a king!" they said. "You don't look like a king to us!" They took an old purple robe and made a crown from thorny vines, and they dressed Jesus up like a ragged king and laughed.

They made fun of Jesus because they thought He was a failure, a pretend king. They wanted to make Him angry and taunted Him to show off His power. But Jesus obeyed His Father's will and stayed quiet. His Kingdom was not of this world. What great sorrow for all of us that Jesus was humiliated for our sins!

Let this mystery teach us to accept mockery and scorn for being disciples of the Savior.

Fourth Sorrowful Mystery
The Carrying of the Cross
Matthew 27:32, Mark 15:21, Luke 23:26-32, John 19:17

The high priests and the crowds demanded that Jesus be crucified. Pontius Pilate knew that Jesus was innocent but agreed to impose the death sentence. "Take him away to Golgotha", he told the soldiers. Golgotha was a hill outside the city, where the Romans crucified criminals.

Jesus had to carry the heavy Cross through Jerusalem to Golgotha. He was very tired and weak. The scourging and the crown of thorns made His head and back bleed. Crowds screamed, laughed, and threw things at Him. But Jesus patiently obeyed His Father and carried the Cross for our salvation.

What great sorrow for all of us that Jesus carried His Cross for our sins!

Let this mystery teach us to be patient with our crosses.

Fifth Sorrowful Mystery
The Crucifixion
Matthew 27:33-50, Mark 15:22-37, Luke 24:33-46, John 19:18-30

When Jesus reached Golgotha, the soldiers stripped off His clothes. They nailed His hands and feet to the Cross and put a sign over His head: "Here is the king of the Jews." Then they pushed the Cross upright. The executioners mocked Him, saying: "You call yourself a king, why don't you save yourself!"

Mary and one of the disciples stood near the Cross. Jesus spoke to them, telling them to be faithful to God and each other. He knew that they did not yet understand what God's will was for them and for His Church. He knew that His death would bring salvation to them and the whole world.

What great sorrow for all of us that the cost of our salvation was Jesus' death on the Cross!

Let this mystery teach us to be always faithful to God.

THE CHAPLET of the Seven Sorrows of Mary

This devotion honors the Seven Sorrows of the Blessed Virgin Mary. It is said on a circle of seven groups of seven beads each. Each group is separated with small medals, representing the seven sorrows of Mary's life. The seven sorrows (or dolors—which gave us the girl's name "Dolores") of our Blessed Mother are:

The Prophesy of Simeon in the Temple.
The Flight of the Holy Family into Egypt.
The Losing of the Child Jesus in Jerusalem.
The Meeting of Jesus on the Way of the Cross.
Jesus Suffers and Dies upon the Cross.
Jesus Is Taken Down from the Cross.
Jesus Is Buried in a Tomb.

At each medal, the leader announces the theme for meditation; then all say an Our Father. Seven Hail Marys follow on the group of beads. At the conclusion, three additional Hail Marys are said in remembrance of the sorrowful tears of our Lady.

MARY'S FLOWERS

Iris The deep-blue color of this flower is a traditional symbol of Mary's faithfulness, and the blade-shaped leaves remind us of the sorrows that "pierced her heart". Its older names are "blue flag" and "sword lily". The iris is the "fleur-de-lis" of Quebec and France.

Flower of Jesse's Root; Formed without Sin; Forth-bringer of the Ancient of Days; Forth-bringer of God; Forth-bringer of God; Forth-bringer

The Glorious Mysteries

First Glorious Mystery
The Resurrection
Matthew 28:1-7, Mark 16:1-7, Luke 24:1-7, John 20:1-8

On the morning after the Sabbath, women disciples of Jesus went to the tomb to finish preparing Jesus' body for burial. They were still tired and sad. They had cried all the day before, because of the death of their Lord. When they arrived at the tomb, they saw that the stone was rolled away. Two angels told them, "He is not here. He has risen as He promised." The women ran to tell the disciples and Mary what they had seen and heard.

Soon, everyone had heard the amazing news. Jesus appeared to His disciples and showed them His wounds. What glorious news! Christ is risen and we will have eternal life.

Let this mystery teach us to have a strong faith in God.

Second Glorious Mystery
The Ascension
Mark 16:19-20, Luke 24:50-51, Acts 1:6-11

Jesus spent forty days with His disciples. He taught them to understand the Scriptures and to preach repentance and forgiveness of sins in His name.

Then Jesus led His disciples out of the city. He told them, "I am going to My Father to prepare a place for you." He spread out His hands and blessed them. As He blessed them, He rose into heaven and disappeared from sight. The disciples stared at the sky in awe. Two men in shining white garments appeared, saying, "What are you doing? Jesus has gone to His Father. He will return the same way." What glorious news! Christ is risen and has made a place for us in heaven.

Let this mystery teach us to hope in God's great mercy.

Third Glorious Mystery
The Descent of the Holy Spirit
Acts 2:1-4

Before Jesus ascended into heaven, He promised His disciples that He would send the Holy Spirit. The disciples returned to the city, to the upper room where they were staying, praying and praising God. There, ten days later, a great noise and light filled the room, and the Holy Spirit filled them all with grace and power.

The disciples began preaching in many different languages. They told everyone of the great love and mercy of God. They preached about the forgiveness of sins through Christ's death and Resurrection. Many who heard them were converted that day. What glorious news! Christ is risen and has sent the Holy Spirit to strengthen and guide us.

Let this mystery teach us to spread God's word in our lives.

Fourth Glorious Mystery
The Assumption
Genesis 3:15

Years passed. Christ's Church on earth had grown. The Apostles and disciples traveled everywhere, spreading the good news of God. On the Cross, Jesus had said to His Apostle John, "Behold your mother", thus placing Mary in his care.

Finally, the end of Mary's time on earth came: The Apostles prayed for her as she died, and they laid her in a tomb. Because she was the Mother of the Savior and had herself been without sin, Jesus came and took Mary into heaven to live with Him forever. What glorious news! Our Blessed Mother is in heaven praying for us.

Let this mystery teach us to follow Mary's example and to pray for a holy life and death.

Fifth Glorious Mystery
The Coronation of Mary
Revelation 12:1

Mary lived her life in obedience to God's will. She was always without sin. She bore the joys and sorrows of her mother-hood with trust in God at all times. She is the perfect example of a woman and a mother.

Jesus brought His Mother to heaven. He crowned her as the Queen of Heaven, of all the saints, and of all the Church. She loves and cares for everyone as she loved and cared for Jesus. Jesus listens to her prayers as He listened to her as a child.

What glorious news! The Blessed Virgin Mary will intercede for us, her children, to her Son, our Lord.

Let this mystery teach us to have a great love for the Blessed Virgin Mary.

Chaplet of the Holy Spirit

The chaplet of the Holy Spirit honors the Holy Spirit in the same way the Rosary honors the Virgin Mary. Both are intended to draw the soul closer to God. The Chaplet is a devotion approved by Pope Leo XIII in 1902.

The devotion begins with the Sign of the Cross, an act of contrition, and a hymn to the Holy Spirit, using three small beads.

Next are five groups of seven small beads between two large beads. These five groups represent the five mysteries of the Holy Spirit and the five wounds of Christ, the means by which the graces of the Holy Spirit were made available to all people.

In each group, the Glory Be is said on the seven small beads; and an Our Father and a Hail Mary are said on the two large beads.

At the end of the five groups, the Chaplet concludes on the three small beads with the Apostles' Creed, one Our Father, a Hail Mary, and a Glory Be for the intentions of the Holy Father.

The five mysteries of the Holy Spirit are:

The Holy Spirit at the Incarnation

The Holy Spirit at the Baptism of Our Lord

The Holy Spirit Led Jesus into the Desert

The Holy Spirit at Pentecost

The Holy Spirit in the Church Today

The Luminous Mysteries

In *Rosarium Virginis Mariae* (dated October 16, 2002, the beginning of the twenty-fifth year of his Pontificate), John Paul II suggested that five new mysteries may be added to the Most Holy Rosary in order to examine more fully and delve the heart of God's love as lived through the life of Christ. The tremendous importance of this document will likely not be recognized till centuries have passed.

*The Mysteries of Light
according to Pope John Paul II*

"Moving on from the infancy and the hidden life in Nazareth to the public life of Jesus, our contemplation brings us to those mysteries which may be called in a special way "mysteries of light". Certainly the whole mystery of Christ is a mystery of light. He is the "light of the world" (Jn 8:12). Yet this truth emerges in a special way during the years of His public life, when He proclaims the Gospel of the Kingdom. In proposing to the Christian community five significant moments—"luminous" mysteries—during this phase of Christ's life, I think that the following can be fittingly singled out: (1) His Baptism in the Jordan, (2) His self-manifestation at the wedding of Cana, (3) His proclamation of the Kingdom of God, with His call to conversion, (4) His Transfiguration, and finally, (5) His institution of the Eucharist, as the sacramental expression of the Paschal Mystery.

"Each of these mysteries is a revelation of the Kingdom now present in the very person of Jesus."

The First Luminous Mystery
Christ's Baptism in the Jordan

Matthew 3:13-17,
Mark 1:9-11,
Luke 3:21-22

John called the Jewish people to repent and prepare for the coming of the Messiah. He baptized many people in the River Jordan.

John knew that Jesus was the Son of God and our Lord. When Jesus came to be baptized, John said, "I need to be baptized by You, and do You come to me?" But Jesus answered, "Let it be so now; for thus it is fitting for us to fulfill all righteousness." Then the Spirit of God came down on Him, and a voice from heaven said, "This is My beloved Son, with whom I am well pleased." What a great light has come to us! With His baptism, Jesus' divine nature is revealed, and His mission on earth began.

Let this mystery teach us to honor the promises of our baptism.

The Second Luminous Mystery
The Miracle at Cana

John 2:1-12

Jesus, His disciples, and Mary were invited to a wedding in Cana, a town in Galilee. Everyone was happy, eating and drinking. When the servers ran out of wine, Mary told Jesus, "They have no wine." Jesus asked her, "What does this have to do with Me? My hour has not yet come." (Jesus was talking about His Passion.)

But it was time to show His glory and power as the promised Messiah, so Jesus had six water jugs filled with water. When people drank it, they tasted delicious wine. This was the first of His signs and miracles, and when His disciples saw it they believed in Him. What a great light is given to us!

Let this mystery teach us to believe in Jesus, who brings the light of faith and eternal life.

The Third Luminous Mystery
Jesus Proclaims the Kingdom
Mark 1:15, Mark 2:1-13, Luke 7:47-48

Jesus was in Capernaum, preaching and healing the sick. Four men there knew that Jesus could heal their sick friend, if only they could get the man close to Him in the house where He was staying. So they made a hole in the roof and lowered their friend into the house. When Jesus saw what they had done, He marveled at their faith and said to the invalid: "My son, your sins are forgiven!"

The bystanders said, "How can you forgive sins? Only God can do that!"

To prove that He had the authority to forgive sins (because He was the Son of God), Jesus then said to the invalid: "Get up! You are healed." The man was instantly healed, and he got up. What a great light shines on us! Jesus heals us all with His love and forgiveness.

Let this mystery teach us to rejoice in God's mercy and forgiveness.

The Fourth Luminous Mystery
The Transfiguration
Luke 9:28-36

Jesus taught His disciples and the people about the Kingdom of God. He explained that He was going to suffer for our sake and then be raised from the dead. Jesus also prayed every day. One day, He took His disciples Peter, John, and James up a mountain. Suddenly they saw Jesus' face shining like the sun. They saw Him talking to Moses, who had brought the Old Law to the Israelites, and to Elijah, the greatest of the Old Testament prophets. The disciples were surprised—and afraid.

Then a loud voice from heaven said, "This is My son; listen to him." Jesus is our new teacher. His teaching replaces the teachings of Moses and Elijah. What a great light is given to us! Jesus, filled with the light of heaven, came to teach us how to enter the Kingdom of God.

Let this mystery teach us that Jesus is the light of the world.

The Fifth Luminous Mystery
The First Eucharist
Matthew 26:26-29, Mark 14:22-25, Luke 22:15-20, 1 Corinthians 11:23–26

It was time for the Passover feast. Jesus knew that His hour had finally come. So He took bread and blessed it. He gave it to His disciples and said: "Take it and eat; this is My body." Then Jesus took wine and blessed it. He gave it to His disciples and said, "Take this and drink, for this is My blood of the new covenant, which is poured out for many for the forgiveness of sins."

Jesus gave this meal of His Body and Blood to His disciples as the first Eucharist. With the Eucharist, we all share Jesus' Body and Blood and receive forgiveness for our sins. What a great light shines in the world! Jesus gives us a new covenant for the forgiveness of sins and the promise of eternal life.

Let this mystery teach us be thankful for the Eucharist.

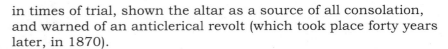

The Miraculous Medal

"O Mary, conceived without sin,
pray for us who have recourse to you."

Saint Catherine Labouré was born in Burgundy, France, on May 2, 1806. Her mother insisted on having her baptized only minutes after her birth, a condition she did not request for any of her other ten children.

At an early age, Catherine entered the community of the Daughters of Charity (also called the Sisters of Charity), in obedience to a vision in which Saint Vincent de Paul told her that God wanted her to nurse the sick. When Catherine was still a novice, only twenty-four years old, the Virgin Mary appeared to her, on July 18, 1830, in the community's motherhouse in Paris.

Going to the chapel on the instructions of an angelic child who had wakened her, Catherine saw a lady seated in a chair to the left of the altar. When Catherine knelt before her and rested her hands in the lady's lap, she was told how to act

in times of trial, shown the altar as a source of all consolation, and warned of an anticlerical revolt (which took place forty years later, in 1870).

A second apparition occurred on November 27 in 1830. The Lady showed Catherine the image that represented the front and back of a medal. The medal was that of the Immaculate Conception, now known as the "Miraculous Medal". Our Blessed Mother asked Catherine to have such medals made and distributed. She told Catherine that wearers of the medal would receive many graces.

At the time, only her confessor knew of the apparitions and instructions that she was receiving. He helped her to have the medals made and distributed, and he kept her identity secret. Devotion to the medal and the Immaculate Conception spread. Not until shortly before her death, in 1876, did anyone else know the identity of the nun who had begun the devotion.

Saint Catherine Labouré died on December 31. Her body was buried in a crypt beneath the motherhouse's church; and, some fifteen years later, it was found to be incorrupt.

In the years since this devotion began, millions of medals have been distributed. Many graces and conversions have been attributed to the wearing of the medal. One of the more famous and dramatic of these conversions is that of the Jewish agnostic Alphonse Ratisbonne.

M. Ratisbonne vigorously denied the importance of God and faith and scoffed at a friend's efforts to bring him into the Church; but, reluctantly, he agreed to wear a Miraculous Medal and pray the Memorare.

While visiting Rome, he happened to visit the church of Sant'Andrea delle Fratte. There, to his surprise and consternation, he saw a vision of the Blessed Virgin exactly as she is represented on the medal. She asked him why he persisted in denying her Son. Alphonse quickly repented and converted.

Saint Maximilian Kolbe, who had a special fondness for the story of Alphonse Ratisbonne, celebrated his first Mass, after his ordination, in the church of Sant'Andrea della Fratte. The story was for him a wonderful example of the love and care of Mary, and also the inspiration for founding the Militia Immaculata movement; wearing the medal and giving it away are integral parts of the movement. He called the Miraculous Medal "a bullet" with which the faithful soldier hits the enemy—that is, evil—and thus rescues souls.

Description of the Medal

The Front   On the front of the medal is an image of the Mother of God, encircled by a banner carrying the prayer: "O Mary conceived without sin, pray for us who have recourse to you."

Mary stands on a globe of the world and on a twisted serpent, the devil. This represents the conflict between good and evil, between Satan and her Son—our Lord, Jesus Christ. She holds her hands out to us, palms outward and down, as if to send heavenly grace into our waiting hearts.

The Back   On the back of the medal is a large letter M with a Cross above it. The M is for Mary and for Mother. She is the Mother of all God's people—a people founded on the twelve Apostles, signified by the twelve stars arranged around the rim. Below the M are two intertwined hearts. These are the hearts of Jesus and Mary. Mary's heart was "pierced by a sword" just as the heart of her Son was pierced by the soldier's spear. The hearts thus joined together are a reminder of God's love for us. As Christ offered Himself on the Cross and Mary stood at His feet, Mother and Son were united in the work of redemption. The medal tells the essential story of our Faith. It is a mini-catechism for everyone who examines it.

MIRACULOUS MEDAL PRAYERS

Saint Maximilian Kolbe's "Miraculous Medal Prayer"

O Mary, conceived without sin,
pray for us who have recourse to you,
and for all who do not have recourse to you,
especially the enemies of the Church
and those recommended to you. Amen.

Prayer of the Miraculous Medal

O Virgin Mother of God, Mary Immaculate,
we dedicate and consecrate ourselves to you
under the title of Our Lady of the Miraculous Medal.

May this Medal be for each one of us a sure sign
of your affection for us
and a constant reminder of our duties toward you.

Ever while wearing it,
may we be blessed by your loving protection
and preserved in the grace of your Son.

O Most Powerful Virgin,
Mother of our Savior,
keep us close to you every moment of our lives.

Obtain for us, your children,
the grace of a happy death;
so that in union with you,
we may enjoy the bliss of heaven forever. Amen.

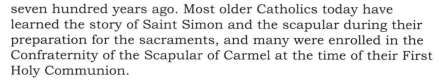

The Scapular

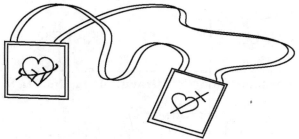

What Is a Scapular?

Originally, a scapular was a cloak or poncho-like garment, usually open at the sides, worn by some monks. A devotional scapular is a modification of this garment, though it is still meant to be thought of as clothing.

Clothing gives protection and shows our station in life. The scapular is also an indication of our spiritual state and a sign of love for Mary. Because Mary's intercession protects us, the scapular is also a sign of protection against the hazards of the world.

The scapular has been reduced from a cloak to two small squares of woven wool, connected by two cords or strings. The squares may have pictures on them. The scapular is worn like a miniature poncho, so that one square is in front and one in back.

There are many different variations of the scapular: white (Trinitarian), black (the Servite Order), blue (of the Immaculate Conception), red (of the Passion of the Sacred Hearts of Jesus and Mary), and green (of Saint Vincent de Paul's Daughters of Charity); but the brown scapular of Mount Carmel is the best known and most commonly worn.

The History of the Brown Scapular

The brown scapular has an interesting and inspiring history.

"Whosoever dies clothed in this shall never suffer eternal fire." The Mother of God made this incredible promise to a Carmelite monk, Saint Simon Stock, in England more than

seven hundred years ago. Most older Catholics today have learned the story of Saint Simon and the scapular during their preparation for the sacraments, and many were enrolled in the Confraternity of the Scapular of Carmel at the time of their First Holy Communion.

As with many other devotions, the devotion of wearing the brown scapular is not commonly practiced among young Catholics. But they embrace this devotion enthusiastically for its immediate and obvious "material" evidence of faith.

One is enrolled in the Confraternity of the Brown Scapular by a priest or other authorized person. When one's scapular wears out, one can replace it.

People who are allergic to wool, live in hot climates, or find the scapular difficult to wear for some other reason can replace it with a **scapular medal**, which has an image of the Sacred Heart of Jesus on one side and an image of Our Lady of Mount Carmel on the other.

Should you decide to practice this devotion as a family, be sure that the children understand that the scapular is not a magical charm to protect you, an automatic guarantee of salvation, or an excuse for not living a Christian life. They need to understand this clearly, not only for their own benefit, but because they will probably be asked or challenged about wearing the scapular by their peers. A scapular can be an excellent opportunity to evangelize!

You could explain that a scapular is like a commemorative T-shirt that you wear to remind yourself of a special occasion, a piece of jewelry like a locket or a charm bracelet that you wear to remind yourself of a loved one, or a special picture that you carry in your wallet to remind yourself of the important people in your life. The scapular reminds us to live as Christians by following the Gospels, receiving the sacraments, and remembering our special devotion to the Blessed Virgin.

Here is what two famous Catholic teachers have said about the brown scapular:

Saint Alphonsus Liguori

"Just as men take pride in having others wear their livery, so the Most Holy Mary is pleased when her servants wear her scapular as a mark that they have dedicated themselves to her service, and are members of the Family of the Mother of God."

Bishop Fulton Sheen

"The Scapular bears a double witness: to Mary's Protection against the ravages of the Flesh occasioned by the Fall, and to Mary's influence as Mediatrix of Graces, who covers our souls with the richness of her Son's Redemption."

Blessing and Investiture in the Brown Scapular

Priest: Show us, O Lord, Your mercy.
Respondent: And grant us Your salvation.
Priest: Lord, hear my prayer.
Respondent: And let my cry come unto You.
Priest: The Lord be with you.
Respondent: And with your spirit.
Priest: Lord Jesus Christ, Savior of the human race, sanctify by Your power these scapulars, which for love of You and for love of our Lady of Mount Carmel, Your servants will wear devoutly, so that through the intercession of the same Virgin Mary, Mother of God, and protected against the evil spirit, they will persevere until death in Your grace. You who live and reign, world without end. Amen.

The priest does the aspersion and invests the person, saying:
Receive this blessed scapular and beseech the Blessed Virgin that through her merits, you may wear it without stain. May it defend you against all adversity and accompany you to eternal life. Amen.

After the investiture, the priest continues:
I, by the power vested in me, admit you to participate in all the spiritual benefits obtained through the mercy of Jesus Christ by the Religious Order of Mount Carmel. In the name of the Father, and the Son and the Holy Spirit. Amen.

May God Almighty, the creator of heaven and earth, bless you, He who has deigned to join you to the Confraternity of the Blessed Virgin of Mount Carmel; we beseech Her to crush the head of the ancient serpent so that you may enter into possession of your eternal heritage through Christ our Lord.

Respondent: Amen.

The Green Scapular

The green scapular can bring protection and increased devotion to Mary and her Son, especially to a lukewarm or disbelieving person. It is often worn as an invocation for cures and conversions.

Our Blessed Mother appeared to Sister Justine Bisqueyburu of the Saint Vincent de Paul Sisters of Charity in 1840, carrying the green scapular. She said, "This holy badge of my Immaculate Heart is to be the means of conversion of souls." Over the course of six years, Our Lady appeared to Sister Justine many times, answering all her questions about the green scapular.

The green scapular does not require a special blessing or enrollment. It should be worn, carried, or placed in the clothing, bed, or room of the person for whom you wish an increase of faith. The Virgin Mary emphasized to Sister Justine that graces received through this devotion are proportionate to the confidence of the donor.

Every day, someone (if not the recipient, then the donor) should say the prayer:

> *Immaculate Heart of Mary,*
> *pray for us*
> *now and at the hour of our death.*

The Sodality of the Children of Mary Immaculate

The History of the Children of Mary

The Sodality of the Children of Mary Immaculate began at the same time as the devotion to the Miraculous Medal. (The word "Sodality" means a lay association formed to carry on devotional or charitable activities.) As devotion to the medal spread, various associations were formed to assist and encourage devotion to the Virgin Mary among young people and children.

One of these was an organization dedicated to Mary Immaculate, for young girls attending the schools run by the Saint Vincent de Paul Sisters of Charity. (Sister Catherine Labouré, who received the apparitions of Mary Immaculate and was entrusted with the medal, and also Sister Justine Bisqueyburu, who received the green scapular, were Sisters of Charity.) The aim was to assist and encourage children to come to know Jesus Christ as our Lord and Savior through devotion to His Mother. Through membership, children learned to pray, to sacrifice, and to practice the virtues, especially purity and modesty.

A letter written by Pope Pius IX in 1876 opened membership in the "Children of Mary" to children not attending the schools or workrooms of the Sisters of Charity. Pope Leo XIII confirmed this permission in 1897 and 1903.

The badge adopted by the Children of Mary Immaculate is the Miraculous Medal, worn suspended from a blue ribbon. Members are encouraged to wear a scapular also.

The Children of Mary Today

Membership in the Children of Mary was very common early in the twentieth century. Many Catholics today still remember their membership with fondness and with an awareness of how much it contributed to their spiritual formation.

Such a memorable tradition deserves reviving. A family or group of families could begin a Children of Mary group in their parish, or as part of their homeschooling activities.

Children of Mary is most suitable for boys and girls between the time of their First Communion and their teen years (ages eight to twelve). A Children of Mary group should not resemble a catechism class (though catechism texts could provide useful material). Instead, plan activities like praying the Rosary, learning devotional songs, and creating and acting in skits recalling events in Church history (especially those involving Mary). Craft projects, such as making rosaries to send to missions, drawing devotional pictures, and volunteering to plant flowers at the church or senior citizens' home, are very suitable for Children of Mary.

Upon joining the Children of Mary, each child says this traditional pledge:

I, [name], a member of the Sodality of the Children of Mary, promise to love, honor, worship, and consecrate my life to the most Holy and Blessed Trinity, the Father, the Son, and the Holy Spirit.

I promise to love our Blessed Mother, to pray the Rosary every day, and to wear the scapular. I promise to encourage unity of our family by praying the Rosary together every day and to remind them that the family that prays together, stays together.

I promise to attend Holy Mass every Sunday and spend as much time as possible in adoration of the Holy Eucharist.

I promise to be a good and obedient child, to keep myself pure and innocent, and to avoid the occasions of sin.

I promise to love Jesus with all my heart, to love our Blessed Mother, and to love and honor Saint Joseph.

I promise to receive the Holy Eucharist as often as I can and to attend Mass on the First Sunday of each month with the Sodality of the Children of Mary.*

---

* If it is not practicable for your children to observe this last promise, you may wish to omit it, or emphasize to your children that, even if they are attending Mass "alone", our communion with the entire Body of Christ means that we are celebrating Mass with the entire Church, and therefore with other Children of Mary, every time we attend.

Marian Saturdays

Five First Saturdays

By the ninth century, a popular veneration of Mary on Saturdays had developed. As Sunday Mass is a weekly celebration of Christ's death and Resurrection, so Saturday is commonly observed as the day of the week when all but Mary succumbed to doubt and despair. Tradition held that Mary alone firmly maintained her faith in her Son and in God. Saturdays, then, were seen as the most appropriate day to honor Mary's steadfastness and faith in her Lord.

The First Five Saturdays—a devotion recommended in 1925 to Sister Lucia (then the remaining survivor of the three Fatima children) in an apparition from Mary—is similar to a novena (nine days of prayer). The First Five Saturdays devotion is prayer offered to comfort Mary's Immaculate Heart and make reparation for all the wrongdoings of men.

Mary made to Sister Lucia her "Great Promise", saying:

> *My daughter, behold my Heart in the midst of thorns that ungrateful persons, at every instant, press on, with their blasphemy and ingratitude. At least you console me. Tell all men that I promise to help, in the hour of their death, with graces necessary for salvation whoever on the first Saturday of each month for five consecutive months will go to confession, receive Holy Communion, say five decades of the Rosary, and keep me company for fifteen minutes in meditation on the Mysteries of the Rosary, with the intention of making reparation to me.*

Fasting on Saturdays

In the very early Christian Church, the practice of fasting continued the Jewish custom of fasting two days each week—on Friday, the day of Christ's death, and Wednesday, the day when Judas made his contract of betrayal with the chief priests of Jerusalem.

In the fourth century, Saturday was added as a weekly fast day, extending the Friday fast, recalling that the Apostles spent the

first Holy Saturday in a state of sadness and fasting. This Saturday fast spread through the Latin Church but was not adopted in the East.

> *The late Father John Hardon explained in one of his talks that his mother never served meat or dessert on Saturdays, an observance that obviously made a favorable and lasting impression on a hungry, growing boy!*

Paint It Blue!   Blue is the liturgical color of Marian feasts. Many flowers named for Mary are blue. Why not honor Mary by painting your front door blue? Like planting a garden, or creating a family prayer corner, a blue door is a very informal devotion, one easily adapted to any circumstance. But like consciously creating beauty for the glory of God and in honor of Mary, or deliberately setting aside a space in your home for prayer and contemplation, painting your door blue in honor of Mary (and saying so when asked) can have a profound effect on both your family and your visitors.

MARY'S FLOWERS

Carnation   The pink or red color of this flower symbolizes love and life, while the spicy fragrance reminds us of the spices the women brought to the tomb of our Lord. The name "carnation" also suggests the Incarnation of Christ.

Rose   Considered the "queen of flowers", the rose is the flower most strongly associated with the Queen of Heaven. It is also seen as a symbol of perfect love (as Mary's was and is). The color, fragrance, and thorns remind us of Mary's role in salvation history. She was faithful and pure. Her Son, our Savior, was crowned with thorns and shed His blood on the Cross for love of all mankind. The thorns of a rose bush also remind us of the fiery thorn bush from which God once spoke to Moses. Mary is the new "rose bush", the miraculously and immaculately conceived means through which God spoke to His people by becoming flesh and dwelling among us.

Argentina, and appeared in Lujan); Our Lady of Madhu; Our Lady of Mariazell; Our Lady of Mercy; Our Lady of

Crowning Mary

Mary's Coronation

In the Marian Year of 1987, the Congregation for Divine Worship published "The Order of Crowning an Image of the Blessed Virgin Mary":

The queen symbol was attributed to Mary because she was a perfect follower of Christ, who is the absolute "crown" of creation. She is the Mother of the Son of God, who is the messianic King. Mary is the Mother of Christ, the Word Incarnate. . . . "He will be great and will be called Son of the Most High; the Lord will give him the throne of his father David; and he will reign over the house of Jacob forever; and of his kingdom there will be no end" (Luke 1:32-33). Elizabeth greeted the Blessed Virgin, pregnant with Jesus, as "the Mother of my Lord" (Luke 1:41-43). Mary is the perfect follower of Christ. The maid of Nazareth consented to God's plan; she journeyed on the pilgrimage of faith; she listened to God's Word and kept it in her heart; she remained steadfastly in close union with her Son, all the way to the foot of the Cross; she persevered in prayer with the Church. Thus, in an eminent way she won the "crown of righteousness" (2 Tim 4:8), the "crown of life" (Jas 1:12; Rev 2:10), the "crown of glory" (1 Pet 5:4) that is promised to those who follow Christ.

The Symbolism of Crownings

Crowns and wreaths are used to signify special status and to ornament a person or object. They are circular, symbolizing eternity, and are frequently made of greenery (or imitations of greenery in precious metals and gems), which symbolizes life.

Kings, queens, and our Blessed Mother are crowned. Brides and grooms in Eastern-tradition weddings and Greek athletes are honored with wreaths or crowns of greenery and flowers.

We hang wreaths on our doorways at Christmastime, and pictures and icons are frequently crowned or ornamented with elaborate frames.

Mary Crowning

The crowning of a statue of Mary, followed by a procession with the crowned statue, is yet another neglected tradition that is worth reviving. The teaching power of these ceremonies for young children and adults alike cannot be overestimated.

Such crowning ceremonies usually take place in May, which is known as Mary's month. In the northern homisphere, flowers are in bloom, the weather is usually suitable for an outdoor event, and everyone is feeling hopeful and lively after a long winter. What better time for us to honor and thank Mary for her love and protection?

The Mary crowning involves placing a statue of Mary on a suitable stand or platform, singing some hymns in her honor, and placing a wreath made of flowers on her head. Other flowers are then laid at her feet. (If possible, a Marian shrine should be kept supplied with fresh flowers all through the month of May.)

If you have a Mary Garden, a simple crowning ceremony could accompany the placing of your statue of Mary in the garden for the summer.

A crowning ceremony is appropriate also on the Feast of the Queenship of the Blessed Virgin Mary, on August 22.

The practice of laying flowers before Mary's statue is deeply embedded in Christian tradition: some Catholic brides lay their wedding bouquets before a shrine of Mary after the wedding ceremony, and pray to her for a blessing on their marriage.

Gardening for Mary

Besides being planted with "Mary's name" flowers, Mary Gardens contain a small statue of Mary, have flowers or stepping stones laid out in the shape of a rosary, or include a bench for quiet contemplation.

Marigolds, virgin's bower, lady slippers, morning glory (also known as lady's mantle), bleeding heart, and roses—beautiful, fragrant flowers have been associated with our Blessed Mother for centuries. Many flowers, especially blue flowers, have a "Mary's name". Forget-me-nots (a lovely name to begin with) are also called "Eyes of Mary". Cornflower (or chicory) is also called "Mary's Crown".

Devotions are activities that, as part of our lives, are intended to affect and improve them. While a Mary Garden is usually only part of a garden, all of our gardening can be a devotional activity, since all of it is devoted to making our surroundings beautiful and is therefore honoring God's creation. Using the produce of your garden to decorate a family altar or prayer corner is an appropriate extension of this idea.

Gardening is a whole family activity, from planning what to grow, laying out the beds, turning the soil, planting seeds and seedlings, to watering, weeding, trimming, and finally harvesting cut flowers and vegetables. Children thus gain an appreciation for the beauty and bounty of God's creation when they help with the gardening—some even begin to enjoy eating vegetables.

While children can help with all the gardening, they enjoy having a garden plot of their own. Some children choose to grow only flowers, though most like to try growing vegetables as well. Here are some and easy-to-grow flowers and vegetables for children:

Flowers

Marigolds ("Mary's Gold") start easily from seed indoors in the early spring, or by planting seeds directly into the garden. There are hundreds of varieties to choose from.

Nasturtiums ("Saint Joseph's Flower"): plant the seeds directly into the garden when the soil is warm.

Impatiens (Mary name: Mother Love!) grow to nicely rounded plants covered with flowers. They will tolerate sun but do best in a shady spot.

Sunflowers (Mary name: God's Eye) take a bit of work but are very exciting to watch as they grow. Feed them well, give them lots of sunlight and water, and before long you may need a six-foot stake to hold them up!

Vegetables

Bush beans produce lots of beans in about two months. Scarlet runner beans will happily climb up a tepee of bamboo stakes (the six-foot ones from the garden store), making a good hide-out!

Cherry tomato plants, either started from seed or purchased at the nursery, will be loaded with small, sweet tomatoes, perfect for eating straight from the plant.

Zucchini is spectacular. Not as fussy as pumpkins and cucumbers, the plants spread amazingly, producing lots of squash—and there will always be at least one giant zucchini discovered at the end of the season.

Onion sets go directly into the soil and put up green sprouts in a few weeks.

Potatoes are also exciting plants to grow, believe it or not. Cut a few grocery-store potatoes into sections, making sure that each section has an "eye". Plant them in sandy, loose soil and leave them alone. In the fall, you will have an amazing "treasure hunt" as you dig up new potatoes with your hands.

Carrots are classic children's vegetables. Though it takes the right kind of soil and growing conditions to get perfect carrots, it is still fun to peek at a carrot in your own garden, to see how big it has grown, or just to pick it, wash it, and eat it.

MARY'S FLOWERS

Ivy Evergreen and vigorous, ivy is a symbol of eternity and faithfulness.

Assumption; Our Lady of the Cape; Our Lady of the Gulf; Our Lady of the Hermits; Our Lady of the Highways; Our Lady

Songs in Mary's Honor

Ave Maria Stella

Hail, bright star of ocean,
God's own Mother blest,
Ever sinless Virgin,
Gate of heavenly rest.

Taking that sweet Ave,
Which from Gabriel came,
Peace confirm within us,
Changing Eva's name.

Break the captives' fetters,
Light on blindness pour,
All our ills expelling,
Every bliss implore.

Show thyself a Mother;
May the Word Divine,
Born for us thine Infant,
Hear our prayers through thine.

Virgin all excelling,
Mildest of the mild,
Freed from guilt, preserve us,
Pure and undefiled.

Keep our life all spotless,
Make our way secure,
Till we find in Jesus
Joy for evermore.

Through the highest heaven,
To the Almighty Three,
Father, Son and Spirit,
One same glory be. Amen.

Hail, Queen of Heaven

Hail, Queen of Heav'n the Ocean Star!
Guide of the wanderer here below!
Thrown on life's surge we claim thy care,
Save us from peril and from woe.
Mother of Christ! Star of the Sea!
Pray for the wanderer, pray for me.

O gently, chaste and spotless Maid,
We sinners send our prayers through thee;
Remind thy Son that He has paid,
The price of our iniquity.
Virgin most pure, Star of the Sea,
Pray for the sinner, pray for me.

And while to Him who reigns above
In Godhead one, in Persons three;
The source of life, of grace, of love,
Homage we pay on bended knee,
Do though O Queen, Star of the Sea,
Pray for thy children, pray for me.

Additional hymns and prayers honoring the Blessed Mother:

Immaculate Mary: The Lourdes Hymn
—see page 31
Magnificat
—see page 36
The Memorare
—see page 37
Flos Carmeli
—see page 38
Salve Regina
—see page 42
Fatima Prayer
—see page 45

Marian Feasts

Celebrating Marian Feasts

Before we are born, our mothers are our entire world; they enfold, nourish, and protect us. When we are born they continue to care for us, by comforting, nursing, and teaching us as we grow. Mothers do not stop being mothers just because we are grown. Our mother will always be our mother.

So it is with our Blessed Mother, the Virgin Mary. She will always be Jesus' Mother, and she will always be our Mother. And if, for whatever reason, our own birth mother is not quite all we would like her to be, our Blessed Mother stands ready, arms open to take us in. As our Mother, she will continue to nourish, protect, comfort, and teach us as we grow. She can be a part of our families and our lives. Daily prayers that greet and thank her for her love and care, and intercessory prayers that ask for her aid, ensure her place in our families, our homes, and our hearts.

She is the *Theotokos* (Greek *theos*, God; *kotos*, bringing forth), the Queen of the Saints, the humble spouse of the Church, and attentive patron of hundreds. (See CCC no. 495.) It is not surprising that there are so many feast days dedicated to Mary.

People around the world have embraced some of these feasts as their own—and there are many other, local celebrations—and special traditions and observances are passed on from generation to generation. For example, Portugal pays special attention to the Feast of Our Lady of Fatima, and Mexico to the Feast of Our Lady of Guadalupe.

Each of these celebrations includes a period of preparation, special decorations, and a Mass. These should remain at the heart of our celebrations, too.

A three-day period of preparation for such celebrations (a *triduum*) is traditional, much like the three-day Easter Triduum, from Holy Thursday to Holy Saturday. Typical observances include a reference to the coming feast in evening prayers, and then some small sacrifice (such as abstaining from meat or sweets) during the three days prior to the feast, so that, when it comes, it is even more festive!

Beyond these bare outlines, let your imagination and your family circumstances be your guide. A procession seems like a good idea? Crowning your statue of Mary with tinsel in January and flowers in August appeals to the children? Why not?

Family Blessing for Marian Feasts

May the Blessed Virgin Mary watch over us and protect us. Through her, God has given us the author of life, Jesus Christ our Lord. By her example may we grow closer to Him, who is Lord of all. Amen.

Saturday Masses of the Blessed Virgin Mary

It is not possible to commemorate all the "names of Mary" in the year, so only the major feasts of Mary are included in the Roman Calendar.

But, since the 1500s, permission has also been given to celebrate a Saturday Mass in honor of our Lady on any Saturday that is not the day of another major feast. Pope Paul VI recommended this practice as "an ancient and simple commemoration." After Vatican Council II, several new Masses were written to extend and expand this veneration of our Lady. Some are specifically intended for use at a particular Marian shrine, others for Saturday Masses. Therefore, on a Saturday when no particular Mass is specified, you could ask your parish priest to celebrate a votive Mass in honor of Mary, using readings from the Common of the Blessed Virgin Mary in the Lectionary:

First Reading (outside of Easter Season)

Genesis 3:9–15, 20
Genesis 12:1–7
2 Samuel 7:1–5, 8–11, 16
1 Chronicles 15:3–4, 15–16; 16:1–2
Proverbs 8:22–31
Sirach 24:1, 3–4, 8–12, 19–21
Isaiah 7:10–14; 8:10
Isaiah 9:1–6
Isaiah 61:9–11
Micah 5:1–5a
Zechariah 2:14–17

First Reading (during Easter Season)

Acts 1:12–14
Revelation 11:19a; 12:1–62, 10ab
Revelation 21:1–52

Responsorial Psalm

1 Samuel 2:1, 4–5, 6–7, 8
Judith 13:18, 19, 20
Psalms 45:10–11, 13b–14, 15–16
Psalms 113:1–2, 3–4, 5–6, 7–8
Luke 1:46–47, 48–49, 50–51, 52–53, 54–55

Gospel

Matthew 1:1–16, 18–23; or Matthew 1:18–23
Matthew 2:13–15, 19–23
Matthew 12:46–50
Luke 1:26–38
Luke 1:39–47
Luke 2:1–14
Luke 2:27–35
Luke 2:41–52
Luke 11:27–28
John 2:1–11
John 2:15b–19
John 19:25b–27

MARY'S FLOWERS

Baby's breath   The tiny white blossoms symbolize innocence, purity, and the breath of the Holy Spirit.

Blue columbine   The columbine (from the Latin word for "dove", *columba*) has a circle of irregular-shaped petals, thought to resemble doves. Doves symbolize both the Holy Spirit and peace. Combined with Mary's signature color of blue, the blue columbine is seen as a symbol of fidelity. It often appears in paintings of Mary.

That Bore the Sea; Suppliant for Sinners; Tabernacle of God; Tabernacle of the Word; Temple Divine; Temple Indestructible; Temple of the Lord's Body; Throne of the King; Tower of

Eve; Singular Vessel of Devotion; Sister and Mother; Spiritual Vessel; Spotless Dove of Beauty; Star of the Sea; Star

Solemnity of Mary, Mother of God

January 1

About the Feast Mother of God is Mary's highest title and the source of all her other titles and roles in the Church. From all eternity, God chose the Virgin of Nazareth to be the Mother of His Son. With her "fiat" at the Annunciation, she became the *Theotokos*, the Mother of God (CCC no. 495). At Calvary, God, in the person of Christ, gave His Mother to all mankind as our spiritual Mother, so that through her we might come to Him, as through her He came to us.

In A.D. 431, the third general council of the Church at Ephesus (the Council of Ephesus) defined as Catholic dogma that the Blessed Virgin is the Mother of God (*Theotokos*); the Council also reasserted the teaching of the truth that there is but one divine person in Christ.

In 1931, in honor of the fifteenth centennial of the Council of Ephesus, Pope Pius XI declared the Feast of the Maternity of Mary to the whole Church. The original date for this feast was October 11; it was later moved to January 1, a date associated with honoring Mary since the fifth century in Rome. The feast became known as the Feast of the Circumcision, because Jesus was circumcised on the eighth day after His birth. The Solemnity of Mary, the Mother of God, as the feast is now called, is a holy day of obligation and, like all solemnities, has a special liturgy.

Celebrating the Feast This feast blends celebrations for the end of the old year and the beginning of a new year with the end of mankind's waiting for the Redeemer and the dawning of the New Covenant of God. It is celebrated with many popular devotionals.

In some countries, besides attending Mass in the morning, families spend the minutes near midnight saying the Rosary or other prayers. In some places, the church bells ring out at midnight to "ring out the old year and ring in the new", telling everyone who can hear that it is a joyous occasion.

A New Year's Eve gathering of families could re-create this custom for modern times with a night of snacks, singing, games, and videos, culminating in a joyous ringing of handbells, jingle bells, and other bells at midnight, ending with a Rosary. It may be possible to find a church with a midnight Mass.

Many North American families continue a custom brought from the "Old Country" of blessing the family on January 1. The father makes the Sign of the Cross on the foreheads of his wife, children, and other relatives living in the home, saying: *May God bless you and keep you safe in the coming year.*

In an exuberant Ukrainian tradition, children toss handfuls of wheat (gently!) at their parents, while wishing them a healthy and blessed new year. The wheat symbolizes new life in Christ. Some cultures give gifts, especially to children, on January 1 rather than on Christmas Day or Epiphany. This custom was maintained in Scotland and France after Spanish-speaking countries and Italy moved to gift-giving on Epiphany (January 6).

A special family dinner, perhaps with the same guests as at Christmas or the guests who were not able to join you at Christmas, is a good way to celebrate this feast. The father, grandfather, or oldest male present can give a family blessing before he blesses the food at the beginning of the meal. Each person can then share what he is thankful for in the past year and what he looks forward to in the coming year.

Feast of the Presentation of the Lord (Candlemas)

February 2

About the Feast This feast is my earliest memory of Catholic liturgy. In 1971, my family was living in Glasgow, Scotland. It was my habit to spend Saturdays with my friend Mary-Anne G. On our way to a swimming pool one cold and rainy afternoon in February, Mary-Anne asked if I would mind attending a Catholic Mass with her before going to the pool. I did not mind, so we stopped at the church.

We were met inside the church door by the priest, who was wearing a white robe trimmed with crocheted white lace, and with him were two small boys similarly dressed. The boys held baskets of slender candles and handed one to each person entering the church, which seemed both small and ornate to my Presbyterian eyes.

I remember that the Mass was in some language I guessed was Latin. There was a lot of repeated standing, sitting, and kneeling. My mother had told me that at fancy dinners and strange churches, I should always follow what everyone else was doing, so I stood, sat, and knelt along with everyone else. I remember noticing that there was both peace and a distinct sense of ordinariness—a sense that there was nothing unusual or awkward about this ceremony. For some reason, church on a February Saturday afternoon was just part of normal life to this congregation.

Mass ended, so Mary-Anne and I went swimming. I forgot all about this experience for nearly twenty years, until, while meditating on the Rosary and reading about Jewish law, I connected the historical real event of the "presentation in the Temple" with a specific date—sometime in February. The memory of that cold and rainy Glasgow afternoon flooded back, and I then understood that the seeds of my conversion to Catholicism had been planted very early.

In Jewish law, forty days after the birth of her child, a mother was required to offer a sacrifice of purification before she could resume her normal activities and movement in society. At the same time, the first-born son was to be offered in thanksgiving to God. The Gospel of Luke (2:22-38) describes how Mary and Joseph fulfilled this command of the Law in Jerusalem. They may have remained in Bethlehem or Jerusalem while the Infant was still young, before the flight into Egypt. The Gospel also relates that, while the Holy Family was at the Temple, both Anna and Simeon recognized the Christ Child as the Messiah. This event is the fourth Joyful Mystery of the Rosary.

Celebrating the Feast Because Christ was present at this event, it was instituted as a feast day quite early in the Church's history. The first recorded description of the feast, called the Feast of the Purification, is dated around the year 390. In 701, Pope Sergius I decreed that candles be used in the processions and celebrations of the Feast of the Purification (and three other feasts of Mary: the Annunciation, Assumption, and Nativity of Mary).

Blessing of candles at this feast was instituted about a century later. At the same time, other liturgical blessings of fire, water, and palms were introduced. Candles symbolize Christ: the wax His flesh, the wick His soul. As Christ gave Himself for us, the flame consumes the candle to give us light.

In some countries, families bring large decorated candles, similar to paschal candles, to the church for blessing on this day. After being blessed, these candles are taken home and lit at family feasts, at times of prayer, and at the bedside of the sick.

Candles of at least 51 percent beeswax are specified for use in the Church because beeswax candles are considered the sweetest and purest, the most appropriate type for symbolizing the humanity of Christ.

From this blessing of the candles, the Feast of the Presentation of the Lord gained its alternate names Candlemas (English), Chandeleur (French), Candelora (Italian), Candelas (Spanish), Lichtmess (German), and Svijetlo Marijino (Light Feast of Mary: Yugoslavian).

Our Lady of Lourdes

February 11

About the Feast On February 11, 1858, the first of the apparitions of Mary to fourteen-year-old Bernadette Soubirous, a peasant girl, occurred in Lourdes, France. On that day, while the girl was gathering firewood with her sister and friends, she saw "a beautiful Lady" dressed in white, with a rosary hanging from her arm, standing in a small cave-like space (grotto) in a cliff side. The Lady smiled at her and called to her. They prayed the Rosary together. Bernadette said the prayers, and the Lady joined in for the Glory Be.

A week later, on February 18, the Lady asked Bernadette to come to the same place for the next fifteen days. Day after day, Bernadette went to the grotto, and the Lady appeared. Each time, she told Bernadette a little more about who she was. More and more people went with Bernadette. They did not see the Lady, but they could tell that Bernadette was seeing something very special and beautiful, because Bernadette herself looked so happy and beautiful when the Lady was there.

The Lady told her that we all must "pray for the conversion of sinners", do "penance, penance, penance!" and "go tell the priests to have people come here in a procession and to have a chapel built here."

On February 25, two weeks after the beginning of her appearances, the Lady of the grotto told Bernadette to dig in the earth at the base of the cliff. Bernadette did as instructed, and a spring of water appeared, though there had never been any sign of a spring there before. The Lady told Bernadette to drink from it and wash herself in it. And even though the water was still muddy from her digging, Bernadette obeyed. Everyone watching was convinced that Bernadette had gone mad. Many people left and stopped believing that she was really seeing our Lady.

On March 25, the Lady told Bernadette, "I am the Immaculate Conception." Bernadette did not know what these words meant, but she carefully repeated them over and over to herself to remember them correctly. Bernadette went straight to the priest's house and said the words to the village priest. He was very surprised.

The "Immaculate Conception" means that Mary was sinless from the first moment of her existence in her mother's womb. Of course, it was only fitting that the one who was going to be the Mother of God and carry Jesus in her womb be without sin herself. Since the sin of Adam and Eve, Mary is the only human who was created untainted by Original Sin. The Church's declaration that Mary was conceived free from original sin had been made only four years earlier. This teaching was confirmed by our Lady in the grotto of Lourdes (see CCC nos. 491, 493). Our Lady appeared to Bernadette eighteen times in all, from February 11 to July 16.

The flowing spring that Bernadette brought forth at our Lady's command still flows today. Many people visit the shrine of our Lady of Lourdes and take Lourdes water home with them. Many people have been healed of all kinds of illnesses at Lourdes after either drinking the water or bathing in it.

The Feast of the Immaculate Conception is celebrated on December 8.

Celebrating the Feast Lourdes is located in the south of France, in the Pyrenees mountains that separate France and Spain. The food from that area combines characteristics of both French and Spanish cooking. Here is a sample recipe from a meal that Bernadette may have eaten on very special feast days.

Poulet Basques

Ingredients

Roasting chicken (two to three pounds)
1 tablespoon salt (half for inside of chicken, half for outside)
black pepper (to taste)
¼ cup olive (or vegetable) oil, for browning
¼ cup butter, melted
3¼ tablespoons rosemary, rubbed to powder (or ½ cup fresh rosemary)
2 sweet red peppers, thinly sliced
3 tablespoons tomato paste
1 medium onion, thinly sliced
3 leeks or green onions, thinly sliced
1 garlic clove (or more to taste), crushed
3 tablespoons diced spicy sausage (such as salami)
2 tablespoons brandy (optional)
Finely chopped pimento, or roasted red pepper, for garnish

Directions

Rub the chicken inside and out with salt, black pepper, and 3 tablespoons of the rosemary. (Or place fresh rosemary inside the chicken.)

Brown it well in olive oil in a heavy roasting pan or Dutch oven.

Pour off excess oil. Brush the chicken with melted butter, and cook in a 325°F oven until tender (a probe thermometer should read 140°F). Baste occasionally with the pan juices.

Carve the chicken into serving pieces, and keep them warm in the oven.

Make a sauce by sautéing the sliced red peppers in 3 tablespoons melted butter. When the peppers begin to go limp, add the remaining ingredients (except the garnish) and simmer gently until the vegetables are tender. Add the pan juices, and let the sauce reduce a bit.

Optional: Warm the brandy, and pour it over the chicken pieces.

Pour the sauce over the chicken; sprinkle with garnish.

Serve with rice and a green salad.

Serves four adults.

Immaculate Mary
The Lourdes Hymn

It is not clear who wrote the words for "Immaculate Mary", known also as the "Lourdes Hymn". The music is a traditional French tune, with the refrain added.

Immaculate Mary, your praises we sing,
Who reignest in splendor with Jesus our King.
    Refrain: Ave, Ave, Ave Maria, Ave, Ave Maria.

In heaven, the blessed your glory proclaim;
On earth, we your children invoke your fair name.
    Refrain

Your name is our power, your virtues our light,
Your love is our comfort, your pleading our might.
    Refrain

We pray for our mother, the Church upon earth;
And bless, dearest Lady, the land of our birth.
    Refrain

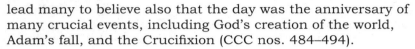
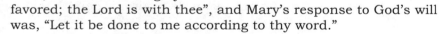
before they came together she was found to be with child of the Holy Spirit; and her husband Joseph, being a just man

Solemnity of the Annunciation

March 25

About the Feast   The Feast of the Annunciation, on the calendar nine months before Christmas Day, is one of the more important feasts of the liturgical year. It commemorates the actual Incarnation of our Savior in the womb of His Mother, Mary. This is the moment when Jesus first "became man and dwelt among us." (See CCC nos. 484–488.)

The biblical account of the Annunciation is found in the Gospel of Luke (1:26-56). Saint Luke describes the moment when the angel Gabriel announced to Mary that she was to become the Mother of God. Luke reports (and tradition holds that Luke probably interviewed Mary herself for this account) that the angel Gabriel first said, "Hail, thou who art highly favored; the Lord is with thee", and Mary's response to God's will was, "Let it be done to me according to thy word."

Despite the fact that Luke's Gospel dates from the first century of the Church—so the actual event of the Annunciation was well known—the Church probably did not celebrate the Annunciation until the early 5th century. It possibly originated at about the time of the Council of Ephesus (c. 431), when Mary was officially declared the Mother of God (see CCC nos. 484–488). (The miracle of Our Lady of Snows is also associated with this Council.) The significance of the Annunciation as the beginning of Christ's life on earth and of our salvation has

lead many to believe also that the day was the anniversary of many crucial events, including God's creation of the world, Adam's fall, and the Crucifixion (CCC nos. 484–494).

It is certainly appropriate for the domestic church to make a special family celebration of this feast. To be profamily is inevitably to be prolife, and the Feast of the Annunciation is a marvelous witness to the sanctity of human life.

In central Europe, farmers honored the feast by putting a picture representing the Annunciation into their barrel of seed grain, and saying a prayer like this one from Austria:

> *O Mary, Mother, we pray to you;*
> *Your life today with fruit was blessed:*
> *Give us the happy promise too,*
> *That our harvest will be of the best;*
> *If you protect and bless the field,*
> *A hundredfold each grain must yield.*

Having asked the help of Mary, they then planted their crops the next day, confident that

> *Saint Gabriel to Mary flies—*
> *'Tis the end of snow and ice.*

Observing the Feast   The Feast of the Annunciation teaches us about the value and sanctity of human life, for God choose to become man in the person of Jesus, the Christ (the Anointed One). It also celebrates Mary's humility, submission, and obedience to God's will, thus bringing such a great gift to us all.

The celebration of the Annunciation and the Incarnation affirms that human life begins at conception, not birth. Many children (and, sad to say, many adults too) think that an individual becomes "real" only at birth, yet the Gospel clearly tells us that Jesus "became flesh" at the Annunciation, not on Christmas Day.

There are several ways we can bring the lessons of the Feast of the Annunciation to our families:

1. A mother fortunate enough to be pregnant at this time can tell her other children that the baby in her "tummy" is already a little brother or sister. This can be a powerful lesson in the truth about human life.

2. When the family is gathered together, either at the dinner table or for evening prayers, read the first chapter of Luke aloud.

3. Parents and older children can read the *Catechism of the Catholic Church*'s section on Article Three of the Creed: "He was conceived by the power of the Holy Spirit, and was born of the Virgin Mary" (nos. 456–511). Use the chapter summary at the end for discussion.

4. Construct an Annunciation scene and put it on display in your home for the week. Use your Christmas crèche figures, and add elements. You might build a "house" from a cereal box or fashion an angel Gabriel to complete the scene.

5. Plant marigold (Mary's Gold) seeds in small pots or paper drinking cups filled with potting soil. Water them gently, and put them on a sunny windowsill to grow.

Remind the children that much of God's work (including our work!) in the world is hidden, just like the marigold seeds, and only eventually flowers into something beautiful after it has had time to grow.

Transplant the seedlings to a flower bed outside when the weather permits.

6. Last but, as far as the children are concerned, not least: Bake a special cake. A seed cake was traditional in England on this feast. An angel-food cake would also be appropriate.

Aside: If you are not in the habit of reading aloud to your children at least once a day, start now! Being read to and seeing parents read for enjoyment are the two most significant factors in promoting a child's literacy!

Seed Cake

Ingredients

2 cups flour
Pinch of salt
½ teaspoon baking powder
¼ teaspoon cinnamon
¼ teaspoon nutmeg
1 cup softened butter
1½ cups white sugar
4 eggs
2½ tablespoons seeds: crushed anise (a licorice taste), caraway (often used in rye or pumpernickel bread), coriander (one of the spices in curry powder), poppy, or cardamom (another curry spice, also used in Scandinavian sweet breads)

Directions

Preheat oven to 325°F. Butter and flour a 7-inch (or 8-inch) springform cake pan.

Sift together flour, salt, baking powder, cinnamon, and nutmeg.

In a deep bowl, cream the softened butter and sugar till fluffy and light colored. In another bowl, beat the eggs till well blended and light in color.

Add one-third of the flour mixture to the butter and sugar. Blend it in well. Add half the beaten eggs, and blend them in thoroughly. Add another third of flour, and blend it in well. Add the remaining eggs and, after blending them in, the remaining flour. Stir in 1½ tablespoons of the seeds, and mix gently until evenly distributed.

Pour the batter into the prepared pan and spread it evenly. Sprinkle the rest of seeds on top of the batter.

Bake in the middle of the oven for about 60 minutes. Use a skewer or thin knifeblade to test the cake for doneness. Remove from the oven when done, and leave to cool for five minutes. Turn the cake out of the pan, and let it cool completely on a wire rack. Wrap the cake in waxed or aluminum paper, and store overnight in the refrigerator. Decorate with a dusting of powdered sugar, or drizzle with icing-sugar glaze.

as the angel of the Lord commanded him; he took his wife, but knew her not until she had borne a son; and he called his name Jesus. *LITANY OF THE BLESSED VIRGIN*

bear a son, and his name shall be called Emmanuel" (which means, God with us). When Joseph woke from sleep, he did

Mary, Help of Christians

May 24

About the Feast   This feast has a recent modern origin, though it stems from the same roots of turmoil, trial, and thanksgiving as have many other titles and feasts of our Lady.

In 1808, Napoleon Bonaparte, the emperor of France, kidnapped and imprisoned Pope Pius VII. He intended to force the Pope to sign a treaty that would grant Napoleon all power over both Church and State in France and all her conquered territories.

From his jail cell, the Pope sent messages to all the Church, calling on the faithful to pray the Rosary for his safe release. The Holy Father also vowed to God that he would institute a special feast in honor of Mary when he returned to Rome and the Vatican.

The eventual collapse of Napoleon's empire forced him to release the Pope; and on May 24, 1814, Pius VII returned to Rome in a joyful and triumphant procession. In thanksgiving, he instituted the Feast of Mary, Help of Christians, in 1815. The feast was added to the calendar of the Papal States, and it was celebrated in other places also, but it is not a feast listed on the calendar of the universal Church.

Patroness of Australia

Only six years later, in 1821, the first Catholic chaplain in Australia, a Father J. J. Therry, dedicated his new parish church to Saint Mary, Help of Christians. The Catholic exiles and settlers there had been praying to Mary, Help of Christians, to send them a priest.

When the first provincial synod of the Church in Australia was held, in 1844, the archbishop of Sydney, the new bishops of Adelaide and Hobart, and approximately half the pioneer priests in the country placed the Church in Australia under the patronage of Our Lady, Help of Christians. The Vatican confirmed this decision in 1852.

The Salesians

Saint John Bosco's love and veneration of Mary, especially under her title "Help of Christians", began early in his life. When he was born, his mother consecrated him to our Lady. When he began his studies for the priesthood, she instructed her son to honor our Blessed Mother and to bring all his difficulties to her. And when he was ordained as a priest, she asked him to take Mary as his Queen.

As a priest, John Bosco took note of the desperate condition of street children in Turin. Despite strong opposition, including attempts on his life by those who wanted to exploit the children as cheap labor, he founded homes and schools for the children.

These schools were the basis of the religious society founded by Saint John Bosco, the Society of Saint Francis de Sales (S.S.F.S.). Some time later, the name of the society was changed to Salesians of Don Bosco, or Salesians for short. Salesian priests today continue to work with and educate boys, under the protection of Our Lady, Help of Christians, and of Saint Francis de Sales.

When poor, abandoned girls began to come to his homes for boys, Father John Bosco founded the Figlie di Maria Ausiliatrice (F.M.A.), with the help of Saint Mary Mazzarello, to care for them. In English, this offshoot religious institute is called Daughters of Mary, Help of Christians.

Perhaps Saint John Bosco's continued devotion to Mary was inspired in part by seeing so vividly the need for a helpful Mother for the children in his care. With his love for Mary and for his fellow man, he would have clearly seen the need for such a Mother for all of us. "The help of God and of Mary will not fail you. . . . I recommend devotion to Mary, Help of Christians, and frequent Holy Communion"—these were the words of Saint John Bosco on his deathbed.

Observing the Feast   The title "Mary, Help of Christians" reminds us of our Lady's constant love for us, her assistance to us, and her call to follow her Son, who said: "Love one another as I have loved you." Charitable service is a perfect way to be a help to each other, as our Lady is a help and comfort to us.

Call a family meeting and ask each other what you might do as a family to help others in need. Sponsor a child in a Third World country? Donate food to a food bank and time to a shelter? Bring all your unused clothing and toys to a charitable organization?

As part of your family dinner or evening prayers on this feast day (after a few days of preparation), consecrate your family home to Our Lady, Help of Christians, and then enjoy these traditional Australian treats.

Consecration of the Home to Our Lady, Help of Christians

Most holy Virgin Mary, appointed by God to be the Help of Christians, we choose you as the Mother and protectress of our home. Favor us with your powerful protection. Preserve our home from fire, flood, lightning, storm, earthquake, thieves, vandals, and every other danger. Bless us, protect us, defend us, keep as your own all who dwell in this home: protect them from all accidents and misfortunes, and obtain for them the grace of avoiding sin. Mary, Help of Christians, pray for us. Amen.

Lamingtons

This Australian tea-time or dessert recipe was reportedly developed in the Queensland Government House kitchen and named in honor of Lady Lamington, wife of the Governor of Queensland, between 1896 and 1901. They are a bit messy but fun to make and eat.

Ingredients

Cake:
  2 eggs
  1 cup sugar
  1 cup cake flour (or all-purpose flour)
  1 teaspoon baking powder
  ½ teaspoon salt
  ½ cup hot milk
  1 tablespoon butter
  ½ teaspoon vanilla extract

Icing:
  2 cups icing sugar
  4 tablespoons cocoa
  2 tablespoons butter
  1 teaspoon lemon or almond extract
  warm water
  2 cups shredded coconut (sweetened or unsweetened)

Directions

Preheat the oven to 350°F. Butter the bottom and sides of an 8-inch square cake pan; then line the bottom with waxed or parchment paper.

Crack the eggs into a large bowl, and beat with an electric mixer for about one minute. Slowly add the sugar, and continue beating until the mixture is very thick and pale. Set aside.

Combine the flour, baking powder, and salt; stir or sift them together well. Set aside.

Heat the milk and the butter just to the boiling point. Slowly pour the hot milk into the egg mixture, while beating at low speed. Add the vanilla, then the flour mixture a small amount at a time, mixing until just blended.

Pour the batter into the prepared pan, and bake for 20 minutes or until a thin knife inserted in the cake comes out clean. Let the cake cool to room temperature in the pan. Cut the cake into 2-inch squares, and let them sit for a few hours to dry out.

To make the icing, sift the icing sugar and cocoa together in a medium bowl. Melt the butter, and add the lemon or almond extract to it. Stir the sugar and cocoa mixture into the butter, and beat well till smooth. Add warm water as needed to bring the icing to a thick, stiff liquid, runny enough to coat the top of the cake pieces but stiff enough not to drip off.

Put the shredded coconut into a shallow tray or bowl. After icing each lamington, dip the top into the coconut while the icing is still moist. Let dry on a wire rack.

Feast of the Visitation

May 31

After the Annunciation, when the angel Gabriel appeared to Mary, she traveled to the village of her kinswoman Elizabeth. Elizabeth's words of greeting to her are included in the prayer we now say as the "Hail Mary".

Luke 1:41–43

And when Elizabeth heard the greeting of Mary, the babe leaped in her womb; and Elizabeth was filled with the Holy Spirit and she exclaimed with a loud cry, "Blessed are you among women, and blessed is the fruit of your womb! And why is this granted me, that the Mother of my Lord should come to me?" (See also CCC nos. 495, 2676-2677.)

Mary responded to her cousin with the words we now know as the Magnificat, recorded in Luke 1:46–55:

And Mary said, "My soul magnifies the Lord, and my spirit rejoices in God my Savior, for he has regarded the low estate of his handmaiden.

"For behold, henceforth all generations will call me blessed; for he who is mighty has done great things for me, and holy is his name.

"And his mercy is on those who fear him from generation to generation. He has shown strength with his arm, he has scattered the proud in the imagination of their hearts, he has put down the mighty from their thrones, and exalted those of low degree; he has filled the hungry with good things, and the rich he has sent empty away.

"He has helped his servant Israel, in remembrance of his mercy, as he spoke to our fathers, to Abraham and to his posterity for ever."

Why is the story of the Visitation included in Luke's Gospel and in the Joyful Mysteries of the Rosary? Is it not because it gives us a glimpse into Mary's character and allows us to

know her more clearly? She demonstrates kindness and charity toward her cousin by going at once to help Elizabeth prepare for the birth of her long-awaited child. This episode shows us her fearless acceptance of God's mission for her.

These are both good reasons. But the Visitation also presents us with a striking preview of what is to come. In this mystery, we see that Elizabeth, who is pregnant with John the Baptist, the last Messianic prophet, greets and rejoices in the presence of Mary, who carries within her Jesus, the Messiah. The Visitation shows us the Old Testament meeting, being fulfilled by, and giving way to the New Testament.

The earliest record of observance of the feast is by the Franciscans in 1263, recommended to them (perhaps as an example of hospitality?) by Saint Bonaventure.

The feast was extended to the entire Church by Pope Urban VI in 1389, near the end of his papacy. The Pope hoped that the intercession of Christ and His Mother would put an end to what is known as the Great (or Western) Schism. This period, which began with Urban VI's election in 1378, saw turmoil and argument over who of two (later three) men was really the Pope and where he should reside. After forty years—and many Church councils, negotiations, and outright conversion of princes, kings, and one "anti-pope"—peace and unity in the Church were finally restored in 1429, with the worldwide recognition of Clement VIII as Pope, and of Rome as his proper residence.

Our Lady of Perpetual Help

June 27

The History of the Icon The traditional picture of Our Lady of Perpetual Help is a Byzantine-style icon, dated to the 13th century. Some records say that the writer of the image (one "writes" an icon) used Saint Luke the Evangelist's portrait of Mary as inspiration.

Painted on wood, it shows the Mother of God holding the Infant Jesus while the archangels Michael and Gabriel fly overhead, holding the instruments of His Passion. His sandal dangles from one foot as if, startled and frightened by the glimpse of His future, the Child has fled to His Mother for comfort. The untied sandal also signifies that Mary alone is "fit to untie His sandal" (see Jn 1:27).

Greek letters over the figures form abbreviated words, naming the Mother of God, Jesus Christ, Archangel Michael, and Archangel Gabriel, respectively.

For many years, the icon was highly venerated on the island of Crete, until the island was conquered by the Turks in the 15th century. Fleeing from the invaders, a refugee from Crete took the holy picture, along with his belongings, and went to Rome.

Another version of the icon's history relates that it was brought to Rome at the end of the 15th century by a merchant. It is unclear whether the merchant bought or stole the image. Either in piety or remorse, he requested in his will that the picture be placed in a church for public veneration. It was taken to the Augustinian church of San Matteo, on the Via Merulana, the pilgrims' route between Santa Maria Maggiore and San Giovanni Laterano. For nearly three hundred years, the image—called Madonna di San Matteo—was the subject of great devotion.

When Napoleon's army invaded Rome in 1812, many churches were destroyed, including San Matteo on the Via Merulana. The icon mysteriously disappeared.

Fifty years later, a monk's mysterious dreams and the explorations of an inquisitive little boy lead to the discovery of the icon, hidden away in the attic of an Augustinian oratory at Santa Maria in Posterula.

Upon hearing of the rediscovery of the icon, Pope Pius IX, who remembered praying before the picture in San Matteo as a small boy, ordered that it should again be displayed on the Via Merulana pilgrims' route. This time, it was housed in the new Redemptorist church of San Alphonsus, built on the ruins of San Matteo. It can be seen there today.

Honoring Our Lady of Perpetual Help

Devotion to Our Lady of Perpetual Help, and veneration of the icon, has been widespread in recent times. Many churches and schools are named in her honor, and reproductions of the image are found in many shrines, churches, and family homes. (See CCC no. 969.)

A common devotion of the 1930s to 1960s was the Novena to Our Lady of Perpetual Help. Many parishes held weekly novenas of prayer to Our Lady of Perpetual Help, offering a sermon, public prayers and hymns, blessing of the sick, benediction, and then veneration of the painting. The devout could attend any nine consecutive services to complete a novena.

Though there are countless prayers composed to Our Lady of Perpetual Help, either to be said privately or as part of a public novena, the well-known Memorare seems most fitting.

The Memorare

Remember, most gracious Virgin Mary,
    that never was it known that anyone
    who fled to your protection, implored your aid,
    or sought your intercession, was left unaided.
Inspired by this confidence, I fly to you,
    O Virgin of Virgins, my Mother.
To you I come; before you I stand, sinful and sorrowful.
Mother of the Word Incarnate,
    despise not my petitions,
    but, in your mercy, hear and answer me. Amen.

Virgin most powerful, pray for us. Virgin most merciful, pray for us. Virgin most faithful, pray for us. Mirror of

Our Lady of Mount Carmel

July 16

Patron of the Carmelites

About the Feast   July 16 is the patronal feast of the Carmelite Order. The Carmelites actually trace their origins back to pre-Christianity, to a community of contemplative hermits who settled on Mount Carmel in honor of the great prophets Elijah and his successor, Elisha.

The hermits' knowledge of Scripture and prophecy inspired them to recognize the Infant Jesus as the Messiah when the Holy Family returned to the village at the base of Mount Carmel—the village of Nazareth—after their two years of exile in Egypt.

Tradition holds that these "Carmelites" were among the first to be baptized by the Apostles into the new Church after Pentecost and that they were the first to take guardianship of the Holy Family's house in Nazareth, following the death of the Virgin Mary and her Assumption into heaven. The hermits built a chapel in her honor there.

The Carmelites did not formally organize themselves as a religious order until the 13th century. At that time they appealed to the Patriarch of Jerusalem to formulate a "rule" for them—a document describing their devotional practices and setting out some rules for the organization and governing of the Order.

The Saracen persecutions during the Third Crusade caused the Carmelites (and a great many other Christians, including the Knights Templar and the Hospitallers) to migrate westward. The Carmelites first reached England in the year 1212. A year later, they were joined by a holy Englishman, Simon Stock.

July 16 was chosen as the Carmelite patronal feast day because on that day in 1251, tradition says, the Blessed Virgin appeared to Simon Stock, then General of the Carmelites, at Cambridge, England. Our Lady showed him the scapular and promised spiritual favors and her special protection to his Order and to all persons who would wear her scapular.

Flos Carmeli

The *Flos Carmeli* (Flower of Carmel) is a prayer composed by Saint Simon Stock. One translation is the following:

> Flower of Carmel,
> Blossoming Vine,
> Splendor of Heaven,
> Mother Divine,
> None like to thee.
>
> Mother of our King,
> Peerless and fair,
> To thy children of Carmel,
> Favors grant e'er.
> Star of the Sea.
>
> *Our Lady of Mount Carmel,*
> *Pray for us. Amen.*

2 Kings 2:11-12   And as they still went on and talked, behold, a chariot of fire and horses of fire separated the two of them. And Elijah went up by a whirlwind into heaven. And Elisha saw it and he cried, "My father, my father! the chariots of Israel and its horsemen!" And he saw him no more.

2 Kings 4:25   So she set out, and came to the man of God [Elisha] at Mount Carmel.

Mark 9:2-4   And after six days Jesus took with him Peter and James and John, and led them up a high mountain apart by themselves; and he was transfigured before them, and his garments became glistening, intensely white, as no fuller on earth could bleach them. And there appeared to them Elijah with Moses; and they were talking to Jesus.

Observing the Feast The history of the Carmelites is closely associated with traveling: Elijah and Elisha traveled the country-side, teaching, preaching, and prophesying; the Holy Family had to make long journeys before returning to their hometown of Nazareth; and the hermits of Carmel traveled from the Holy Land to the West, to England, and eventually to the rest of the world.

In our fast-paced and mechanized world, it is difficult to imagine the challenges and rigors of travel in the past. Without much personal experience of traveling under our own power, how can we possibly comprehend the trust and sacrifice of Joseph and Mary as they traveled, in obedience, first to Bethlehem, then to Egypt, and finally home to Nazareth? The same spirit of trust, sacrifice, and obedience sustained the Carmelites and countless other religious in their journeys.

The fasting of Lent helps us to identify with the poor, especially with those in the Third World. A hiking trip (a pilgrimage on foot) can teach us in a similar way to appreciate our own taken-for-granted blessings. This is a lesson worth learning and teaching our children. So, leave the car in the driveway, and take a trip on foot. Or drive to a nearby wilderness park and take a family hiking trip there. Make it an enjoyable annual tradition, adding the promise of some special treat at the end—toasted marshmallows for the little ones and barbecue for the teenagers.

Such trips build family unity in a way that is as difficult to describe as the ardors of self-propelled travel. In our experience, working together and helping each other through a trip (if one of us does not make it, no one does) teach the meaning of "family" more surely than anything else does.

Self-propelled travel needs lots of preparation. Most of us do not have the experience or physical conditioning to set off on a hiking trip the way someone from the early 1800s might have had. The settlers of the West considered anything over five miles on foot and ten to fifteen miles in wagons a good day's trip, with babies, livestock, farming implements, and household goods in tow, and we can set a similar goal for ourselves.

Start about two weeks beforehand by taking walks as a family around the neighborhood. Gradually add heavy back-packs filled with the clothing, water bottles, and other supplies you will need for your hike. For an overnight trip, consider how you will tote tents, sleeping bags, flashlights, and cooking gear also.

Some rules of thumb for hikers:

Carry essentials only.

- Bring a water bottle for each person (and water-purification equipment if yours is a wilderness trip).
- Bring a well-stocked first-aid kit, plus sunscreen and bug repellent. Check Web sites that list what a first aid kit should contain.
- Bring lightweight, easily digested food, such as pita bread, cheese, dried fruit, juice crystals, and jerky. Peanut butter (carried in a plastic container) spread on pita bread is an excellent source of nutrition for young hikers.

Dress appropriately.

- Wear thick socks and sturdy footwear. Though hiking-boots or -shoes are preferable, running-shoes with a strong, thick sole are fine. (You do not need to buy a whole lot of hiking stuff.)
- Choose clothing based on your expected terrain and temperatures: jeans for cool days, hiking shorts for warm days; jacket or fleece top for cooler evenings; a hat and sunglasses. A walking stick is often the hiker's best friend.

Pace yourself.

- Set yourself some pacing rule, depending on who is in your hiking group. For example: Travel for twenty-five minutes, rest for five. Drink lots of water at each rest stop. Take half an hour for lunch. Sitting for longer will seem appealing, but it just makes it harder to get going again. Don't overshoot the halfway point. Be sure to stop before you are all too tired to get home again!

Queen of apostles, pray for us. Queen of martyrs, pray for us. Queen of confessors, pray for us. Queen of virgins, pray for us. Queen of all Saints, pray for us. Queen conceived

Christians, pray for us. Queen of angels, pray for us. Queen of patriarchs, pray for us. Queen of prophets, pray for us.

Solemnity of the Assumption

August 15

About the Feast   This summer feast honoring our Lady dates from early in Church history. The Feast of the Assumption is first recorded as celebrated by Christians living in what was known then as Palestine (the region around Jerusalem) in about 450.

The feast was originally called the *Koimesis Theokotou* in the Eastern Church and *Dormitio Beatae Mariae Virginis* in the Roman Church (Falling Asleep of the Mother of God).

With the belief that Mary had "fallen asleep" was also the strong conviction that her body did not decay but in some miraculous way had been "assumed" (carried) into heaven. By the seventh and eighth centuries, the feast was known as the *Assumptio Mariae Virginis*. This was such a strongly held tradition in the Church that it wasn't thought necessary to define it as part of the Church's teachings for many centuries.

It was on November 1, 1950, that Pope Pius XII defined as a truth revealed by God that the Immaculate Mother of God, Mary ever Virgin, was taken up to heaven, body and soul, when the course of her life on earth was finished. (See CCC nos. 966, 974.)

Though the origins of both the feast and of the belief in the Assumption of Mary are unclear, it is quite obvious that there are no relics of Mary to be venerated, nor any history of relics now lost.

How Flowers Regained Their Scent

An ancient and beautiful legend about the Assumption of Mary tells the story this way:

When our Lady felt her time on earth coming to an end, she sent word to all the Apostles. They were out preaching the good news of her Son "to all the corners of the world" as Jesus had commanded them. When they received her message, of course they paid their respects to their new congregations

and disciples and left so as to hurry to her side. After long sea voyages and treks over land, they arrived just in time to say goodbye and pray with her one last time. Then she died.

The grieving Apostles took her body to a tomb near the one where Jesus had been laid after His Crucifixion. They covered her with a white shroud and laid her to rest in the tomb.

Only Thomas was late. He had been delayed in some way or another, and had been traveling day and night since to try to catch up. When he finally arrived, hot and travel-stained, he was grief-stricken to learn that she had been laid to rest in a tomb. He wept bitterly, and begged permission to open the tomb so that he could see her beloved face.

At first, the other Apostles were reluctant. After all, she had been dead for three days, and it was a hot country. Finally they yielded to his tears and rolled away the stone.

To their amazement, the tomb was filled with flowers, all giving off a sweet fragrance. The Apostles felt happier and healthier just smelling the beautiful scent that came wafting out of that tomb. Where they had placed her body was only her shroud, filled with more flowers. Her body had been carried up to heaven by her Son and the angels, to join her soul.

Now, it must be remembered that after the great Fall, when Adam and Eve disobeyed God and ate of the fruit of the tree of the knowledge of good and evil, and were cast out of the Garden, all the flowers lost their scent, or perhaps we lost the ability to smell them. The herbs lost their healing powers, too, and they were good only for flavoring our food. Not that that's not a good thing, mind you, but to be able to heal sickness and mend broken bones—well, that's something more important than a nicely flavored stew.

It was only right that on the day of her Assumption, our Blessed Lady's last gift to us should have been the restoring of the scent of flowers and the healing powers of herbs.

—A legend, but a beautiful thought!

Observing the Feast "It is surely fitting, it was becoming, that she should be taken up into heaven and not lie in the grave until Christ's second coming, who had passed a life of sanctity and of miracles such as hers. . . . She died, then, because even our Lord and Savior died. But though she died as well as others, she died not as others die; for, through the merits of her son, by whom she was what she was, . . . which had filled her with light, which had purified her flesh from all defilement, she had been saved from disease and malady, and all that weakens and decays the bodily frame" (John Henry Newman).

In Greece, where the Roman Catholic Church and the Eastern Orthodox Church exist side by side, the Feast of the Assumption (or Dormition) of Mary is an occasion for family gatherings and celebrations. The two weeks leading up to the feast are spent both fasting and traveling home to the family village in time for the feast. It is a pilgrimage, a going home to family, culture, faith, and country for everyone. On the day of the feast itself, the churches are filled with worshippers bringing animals, food, and other offerings. Some churches hold auctions of the offerings to raise money.

For your family, have a "Greek feast" to celebrate the Feast of the Assumption—barbecued lamb chops, fresh crusty bread, a true Greek salad (which has no lettuce), and the classic Greek pastry, baklava, for dessert.

Greek Salad

Ingredients

3 tomatoes, sliced
1 large cucumber, sliced (peeled if desired)
1 medium sweet onion (or 5 green onions), sliced
1 cup black olives, pitted
¾ cup feta cheese, crumbled
1 medium red pepper, sliced (optional)
½ cup fresh basil leaves, finely chopped
salt and pepper, to taste
½ cup olive oil
¼ cup balsamic vinegar (or lemon juice)

Directions

In a salad bowl, combine the tomato, cucumber, and onion. Add the olives, feta cheese, sliced pepper (option), and basil. Sprinkle with salt and pepper; drizzle with olive oil and the vinegar (or lemon juice). Toss. Let sit for about an hour to allow the flavors to mingle. Serve cold or at room temperature. Serves 4 to 6.

Baklava

Ingredients

4 cups walnuts, finely chopped
½ cup white sugar
1 teaspoon cinnamon
1 pound phyllo dough (frozen-food section of grocery stores)
1 cup butter, melted
1½ cups honey, melted
¼ cup rosewater or orange flower water (or ¼ cup water and 1 teaspoon vanilla)

Directions

In a large bowl, combine the chopped nuts with the sugar and cinnamon. Set aside.

Brush melted butter on the bottom and sides of a 13x9-inch baking dish. Place one sheet of phyllo dough in the baking dish (keep remaining sheets covered with a damp tea towel), allowing it to extend up the sides of the dish. Brush the sheet with melted butter. Repeat to make a layer of 5 sheets of phyllo dough. Sprinkle with 1 cup of walnut mixture.

Cut remaining phyllo sheets into rectangles about 13x9 inches. Lay one sheet on top of the walnut mixture, and brush with melted butter. Repeat this layering of walnut mixture and phyllo sheets twice more. You will have three layers of walnut mixture. Top with remaining phyllo sheets, brushing each with butter. Trim off edges of phyllo that extend over the edge of the dish.

With a sharp knife, cut just halfway through all layers to make a diamond pattern of about 28 servings. Bake in a 300°F oven for 1 hour and 25 minutes or until top is golden brown.

Heat honey and rosewater in a saucepan until hot but not boiling. Spoon hot honey evenly over baked baklava. Cool in baking dish at least 1 hour. Cut the rest of the way through diamonds to serve.

Memorial of the Queenship of Mary

August 22

About the Feast Four years after he defined the dogma of the Assumption of Mary, Pope Pius XII, in the encyclical letter *Ad Caeli Reginam*, decreed and instituted the Feast of the Queenship of the Blessed Virgin Mary. He thus acknowledged and made formal a long-standing Church tradition. From the earliest centuries of the Church, belief in Mary's Queenship in heaven had been part of the Christian faith. Though nothing is said directly about either Mary's Assumption or her Coronation in the Bible, these beliefs are based on both scriptural references and tradition.

First, if Jesus is our Lord and King, then surely His Mother Mary is a Queen. "Behold, you will conceive in your womb and bear a son and you shall call his name Jesus. He will be great and will be called the Son of the Most High. . . . Therefore the child to be born will be called holy, the Son of God" (Lk 1:31–35).

Mary is our Mother and Queen inasmuch as "the Son whom she brought forth is he whom God placed as the first-born [Lord and Savior] among many brethren (Rom 8:29), that is, the faithful, in whose generation and formation she cooperates with a mother's love" (*Lumen Gentium*, no. 63).

Mary is the Queen of Heaven inasmuch as, being the new Eve, the one who obeyed, she is the "woman" described in Revelation: "A great sign appeared in the sky, a woman clothed with the sun, with the moon under her feet, and on her head a crown of twelve stars" (12:1).

By first carrying her to heaven, then crowning her in the sight of all the angels and saints, God richly rewarded his most faithful of servants. Mary's own prophecy was fulfilled: "Truly all people shall call me blessed, for the Lord has done great things for me."

Salve Regina

The text and music of this song are based on the Latin prayer *Salve Regina*. This is the common English version of the song.

Hail! holy Queen enthroned above, O Maria!
Hail! Mother of Mercy and of love, O Maria!

> *Refrain*:
> Triumph, all ye cherubim,
> Sing with us, ye seraphim.
> Heav'n and earth resound the hymn.
> Salve, salve, salve Regina!

Our life, our sweetness here below, O Maria!
Our hope in sorrow and in woe, O Maria!
Refrain

To thee we cry, poor sons of Eve, O Maria!
To thee we sigh, we mourn, we grieve, O Maria!
Refrain

This earth is but a vale of tears, O Maria!
A place of banishment, of fears, O Maria!
Refrain

Turn then, most gracious advocate, O Maria!
Toward us thine eyes compassionate, O Maria!
Refrain

When this our exile is complete, O Maria!
Show us thy Son, our Jesus sweet, O Maria!
Refrain

O clement, gracious, Mother sweet, O Maria!
O Virgin Mary, we entreat, O Maria!
Refrain

Feast of the Birth of Mary

September 8

About the Feast Tradition holds that Mary was the only child of Saint Anne and Saint Joachim, whose feast day is celebrated on July 26. Though there is no record of Mary's actual day of birth, this feast was celebrated by Christians in Syria and Palestine as early as the sixth century, when on a particular September 8 a church in Jerusalem was consecrated in Mary's honor.

Over the next several centuries, observance of this feast spread to the Western Church; by the Middle Ages, it was a public holy day and remained a day of obligation until 1918. (The Feast of the Annunciation also was removed as a day of obligation at that time.)

In many central and eastern European countries, September 8 is associated with thanksgiving and harvest festivals and blessings of the seed for next year's crops. In France, vineyard owners offer their best grapes to "Our Lady of the Grape Harvest".

Observing the Feast In order to shift children's focus away from Santa-based materialism, many people suggest that Christmas Day be celebrated as a birthday party for Jesus, complete with birthday cake and singing of "Happy Birthday". On September 8, a celebration in honor of Mary's birthday is just as appropriate. And what better cake for such a celebration than angel food cake?

Chocolate Angel Food Cake

A chocolate angel food cake is not traditional, but it's even more delicious than the original.

Ingredients

1 cup sifted all-purpose flour (sift before measuring)
¼ cup cocoa
1¾ cups white sugar
1¾ cups egg whites (reserve the yolks to make a custard)

1½ teaspoons cream of tartar
¼ teaspoon salt
1 teaspoon vanilla

Directions

Preheat oven to 375°F. Place the baking rack at the bottom third of your oven.

Sift together the flour, cocoa, and ¾ cup of the sugar at least twice and set aside.

In a large mixing bowl (it must be ceramic or metal, not plastic), beat the egg whites, cream of tartar, salt, and vanilla until soft peaks form. (The peaks will droop when the beaters are lifted.) Gradually add the remaining 1 cup sugar. Continue beating until stiff peaks form.

Sift about a third of the flour mixture over the egg-white mixture, and gently fold it in with a large rubber spatula instead of a spoon. Repeat with the remaining flour, a third at a time. Turn mixture from the bottom of the bowl to the top until there are no streaks of chocolate or egg white, without "deflating" too many of the egg-white bubbles.

Gently spoon the batter into an ungreased 9- or 10-inch tube pan. Run a knife through the batter to remove any large air pockets. Smooth the top of the batter.

Bake for 40 to 50 minutes, until the cake is risen, dry looking, and slightly brown.

Cool by placing the tube pan upside down—inverted on a wine bottle (or other narrow-neck glass bottle) if your pan does not have little "feet" to hold it off the counter. Allow the cake to cool completely before removing it from the pan.

Serve by topping slices with a thin chocolate sauce or chocolate-flavored whipped cream (whipped cream with cocoa and sugar added).

Memorial of Our Lady of Sorrows

September 15

About the Feast The Church has always had a profound sympathy for the sufferings of Mary during her Son's Passion. "Standing by the cross of Jesus were his mother, and his mother's sister, Mary the wife of Clopas, and Mary Magdalene" (Jn 19:25). Even if we cannot fully comprehend the agonies of Christ, we can certainly identify with Mary's grief and sorrow.

But formal recognition of the *sorrows* of our Lady, in the form of a feast day, did not come until the twelfth century. Once the feast was instituted, and promoted by the Cisterians and Servites, the devotion spread quickly throughout the Church. In 1482, the Feast of Our Lady of Sorrows was added to the Roman Missal under the title of "Our Lady of Compassion".

In 1727, Pope Benedict XIII placed the feast on the Roman Calendar, to be celebrated on the Friday before Palm Sunday. In 1913, Pope Pius X set the date as September 15.

In her sorrows, Mary suffered also for all of us—for parents who see their children's pain, for those in pain themselves, for the persecuted or oppressed, for the lonely, the lost, and the abandoned. We can turn to our Mother Mary for strength and comfort when our sorrows seem too much for our hearts to bear.

The Seven Sorrows of Our Lady

1. The prophecy of Simeon
2. The flight into Egypt
3. The losing of Jesus in the temple
4. Mary meets Jesus carrying the Cross
5. The Crucifixion
6. Mary receives the dead body of her Son
7. The burial of her Son and closing of the tomb

Celebrating the Feast This feast occurs approximately six months after the midpoint of Lent, and may take the form of a mini-Lent. Just as Lent is a powerful teaching season for the family (it can open the way to dinnertime discussions of the value of sacrifice and suffering, for example), this feast can refresh our Lenten memories.

Rather than having a "feast" with dessert, we could share a simple meal in the midst of harvest plenty; and our appreciation for such a meal will be heightened.

Assign a "sorrow of Mary" to each member of your family a few days before the meal. Let each one consider the sorrow as it is described in Scripture, as it is similar to a personal experience, and be ready to discuss what it teaches us about Mary as an example for our lives. Even a young child of five or six can participate in this discussion. You may be surprised at the depth and wisdom of your children's contributions.

Mary's Flowers

Gladiolus The name comes from the Latin name for "sword". Its sword-shaped leaves symbolize the "piercing sorrows" that Mary endured. Red gladiolus symbolize martyrdom—as do palm branches, for the same reason. Palm branches are a symbol of victory and, as Christian symbols, represent the martyrs' victory over death.

Memorial of Our Lady of the Rosary

October 7

About the Feast   On October 7, 1571, a Christian fleet composed of ships from Spain, the city-states of Italy, and the Knights of Malta challenged a Muslim Turkish navy for posses- sion of Cyprus, which the Turks had captured a few months before. The battle took place at Lepanto (now known as the Gulf of Corinth), in the Mediterranean Sea.

The Christian fleet, organized and consecrated by Pope Pius V and com- manded by Don Juan, son of Charles V, prayed the Rosary together before enter- ing battle. They achieved a stunning victory, killing thirty thousand Turks (only seventy-five hundred Christians were killed in the battle) and rescuing twelve thousand Christian slaves who had been chained as rowers for the Turkish fleet.

This decisive battle turned back the advancing Muslim forces, who were poised to invade and conquer Europe. All of Christen- dom celebrated. In 1572, on the anniversary of the battle, Pope Pius V instituted this feast in thanksgiving to Our Lady of the Rosary. He invited all to celebrate by meditating on the myster- ies of Christ and following the example of the Blessed Virgin Mary. G. K. Chesterton's poem *Lepanto* gives an exciting and vivid account of this battle.

Observing the Feast   If you do not yet pray the Rosary as a family, this feast day is an excellent time to introduce this devotion to your family. The accounts of the Battle of Lepanto

are sure to capture the imagination of small boys, while the loving care with which our Lady protects us will appeal to small girls, who lavish the same care (they imagine!) on their dolls.

Do not be discouraged if this is the third or fourth or too-embarrassed-to-count time you have tried to institute the family Rosary. Even a daily decade is enough to kindle a spark of Marian devotion in your family—a spark that is sure to grow.

Try praying each decade as Pope John Paul II recommended in *Rosarium Virginis Mariae*, the document in which he also pro- posed the new Luminous Mysteries.

Announce the mystery and read the related scriptural passage aloud. Let the older children take turns reading from the Bible.

Then read a short meditation on the mystery. Meditations can recount the events, focus on the interior state of those present, or call us to meditate on the "fruits" (what it can teach us) of each mystery. Some recommend that the meditation and fruits be considered after praying the decade, but for children, the usual order works best—their patience may be exhausted by the end of the decade.

Finally, pray the decade. Close with a Glory Be and the Fatima Prayer.

Fatima Prayer

When she appeared to Francesco, Jacinta, and Lucia at Fatima, our Lady asked the children to add this prayer to their Rosary.

> O my Jesus, forgive us our sins,
> save us from the powers of hell,
> and lead all souls to heaven,
> especially those in most need of Your mercy.
>   Amen.

Austin, Texas; Australia; Austria; Aviators; Barcelona, Spain; Archdiocese of Baltimore, Maryland; Belgian air crews;

Bolivian navy; Brazil; Diocese of Brooklyn, New York; Builders; Diocese of Burlington, Vermont; Cajuns; California; Diocese of Camden, New Jersey; Canada; Catemaco, Veracruz,

Belgium; Bicycle riders; Bicyclists; Diocese of Bismarck, North Dakota; Blood donors; Boatmen; Bodily ills; Bolivia;

Memorial of the Presentation of Mary

November 21

About the Feast   According to apocryphal sources, this feast was celebrated as early as the second century. Reliable records show that it was observed in the Eastern Church by the sixth century. In 1372, when Pope Gregory XI learned of this feast's being celebrated in Greece, he introduced it at Avignon. Eventually, in 1585, Pope Sixtus extended the feast to the universal Church.

The feast celebrates two events: the presentation of the child Mary in the Temple, which probably occurred when she was three years old; and the consecration of a basilica dedicated to Mary in Jerusalem, built near the site of the Temple.

Mary was the only child of her parents, Saint Anne and Saint Joachim. Though it was not obligatory to present a first-born daughter to the Lord, as it was with a first-born son, many Jewish parents did follow this custom. Girls were presented at about the age of three, whereas boys were presented at a much younger age, at forty days old.

Her presentation at the Temple meant that Mary later probably received an education. That is, she would learn to read sacred Scripture and also to write, in addition to learning traditional feminine skills, such as weaving, sewing, and cooking.

With this in mind, we see the faith and obedience of her "fiat" at the time of the Annunciation as especially poignant and significant, for she would then have been well aware of the prophesies concerning the coming Messiah, including those foretelling His painful Passion and death.

Observing the Feast   We should follow Mary's example so that our "yes" to Christ is as heartfelt and sincere as was hers. Knowledge of the Scriptures will help us. The more we know of "salvation history", the more we will embrace and appreciate the great gift of faith we have been given.

Here are a few family games and activities that will help us to learn the Scriptures. Any one of these games could become a family favorite.

Bible Charades

In teams, or individually, choose an Old or New Testament scene, and, portraying the characters (or animal!) involved, act it out *without words*. Other members of the family try to guess who's who and what's what. As the family becomes more familiar with this game, players will have to read the Bible carefully to find less obvious events and people to portray. "Winning" is correctly guessing the character or event portrayed.

Bible Pictionary ®

This game is a pencil-and-paper version of charades. An event, character, or animal is chosen, then one member from each team draws pictures that help their team members guess the word or phrase. A team "wins" by guessing correctly first. There is a commercial version of this game.

Bible Twenty Questions

One person chooses a character, event, or animal from the Bible; then the rest of the family must guess who or what it is by asking questions that can be answered only "Yes" or "No". "Winning" is correctly guessing the answer before using up all twenty questions.

Feast of Our Lady of Guadalupe

December 12

About the Apparition

On the morning of December 12 in 1531, a poor Aztec Indian man named Juan Diego rose, and made his way through the hills to Mass in Mexico City, as he did every morning.

Juan Diego was 57 years old, a humble and devout Catholic in a still largely pagan country. As he walked the familiar path, Juan thought about his family, his work; and he said a prayer for his sick uncle. Suddenly, he heard beautiful music and a woman's voice calling "Juan, Juan".

Turning from the path, Juan climbed Tepeyac Hill and found a beautiful young Indian woman waiting for him at the top of the hill. She told him that she was the Virgin Mary. When the astonished Juan did not answer, she continued, "Tell your Bishop that I desire a church to be built on this spot. This church will aid the conversion of the Mexican people and be a source of consolation for many."

Leaving the lady, Juan Diego hurried to obey her request. After waiting several hours, he was finally allowed to see the bishop and convey the lady's message. The bishop, perhaps not surprisingly, did not believe Juan. Downcast, the Indian returned to the hill and told the lady what had happened.

"Do not worry, my little one", she replied soothingly. "Return to the bishop and tell him again. All will be well, you'll see." But when Juan visited the bishop again, again the sceptical cleric did not believe his story. Instead, the bishop asked for a sign from the lady to prove that she was, indeed, the Blessed Virgin.

Poor Juan was almost in despair. How could he return to the Lady and report this second failure? But, obedient to the one whom he knew was the Mother of our Lord, he returned to Tepeyac Hill once again.

The Lady provided the requested sign. Beautiful, fragrant roses appeared on the hillside, and, when Juan had gathered them,

Our Lady herself arranged them in his tilma, or cloak. "There, now," she smiled. "Take these roses to the bishop."

In the presence of the bishop for a third time, Juan opened his tilma, and the roses tumbled out at his feet. Awestruck, the bishop fell to his knees. For, in addition to the sign of the roses, there on the inside of Juan's humble tilma was a miraculous image of our Lady.

Soon, a church was built on the site of the apparition, as the Virgin Mary had requested; and within a few years, eight million people had converted to Catholicism.

Guadalupe is the most frequented Marian shrine in the whole world.

About the Tilma

Saint Juan Diego's tilma with its miraculous image hangs to this day in the splendid Basilica of Our Lady of Guadalupe. Although more than 500 years have passed, the coarse cactus fiber shows no sign of disintegration. Examinations of the image have been unable to identify the technique used to create the image.

Many details of the image are significant. Mary is portrayed as a young Indian woman, someone the native Mexicans can see as one of their own.

She is surrounded by rays of light and stands on a crescent moon, as the Woman of the Apocalypse is described in Revelation 12:1: "arrayed with the sun, and the moon under her feet, and upon her head a crown of twelve stars".

Her blue-green mantle is thought to match the color once reserved for the Mexican pagan god and goddess Ometecuhtli and Onecihuatl; and her reddish dress and belt are both associated with pregnancy in Mexican culture.

The stars on Mary's mantle are thought to match the position of some stars in the sky in December of 1531.

All these details create an image of our Blessed Mother that spoke clearly and lovingly to the Aztec natives 500 years ago and speaks just as clearly and confidently to her children today.

The Virgin of Guadalupe had a special role in the evangelization of the Americas. Her importance has been recognized many times. In 1910, Our Lady of Guadalupe was declared the Patroness of Latin America by St. Pius X, and in 1945 Pope Pius XII declared her the Empress of all the Americas.

During his address to the Fourth General Conference of Latin American Bishops in October 1992, Pope John Paul II gave Our Lady of Guadalupe the titles "Star of the First Evangelization" and "Star of the New Evangelization". Later, he wrote, "I welcome with joy the proposal of the Synod Fathers that the feast of Our Lady of Guadalupe, Mother and Evangelizer of America, be celebrated throughout the continent on December 12" (*Ecclesia in America*, 1999). Our Lady of Guadalupe is also called the Patroness of the Unborn.

Celebrating the Feast In Mexico, the festival or celebration of Our Lady of Guadalupe begins in the week before December 12. Families begin to prepare food and decorate their homes; pilgrims begin to travel to Mexico City; some make part of the journey on their knees.

On the evening of December 11, conchero players gather in the atrium of the basilica. (Their name comes from *concha*, "shell", their mandolin-shaped instruments being made from armadillo shells.) The concheros and other musicians begin playing and dancing at midnight and continue all day.

Fireworks are often set off at daybreak. They open the feast day with a bang! Many people also join candlelight processions to their local churches for Mass. They sing *mañanitas*, "morning songs", as they walk.

Las Mañanitas

Las Mañanitas are traditional songs that Mexican people sing early in the morning on special occasions, including the morning of the Feast of Our Lady of Guadalupe. These verses are also sung on the morning of someone's birthday. There are many verses, but here is the most common verse:

English version:

These are the morning verses
That King David used to sing.
Because today is your birthday,*
We are singing them to you.

> *Chorus*
> Awaken, my dear, awaken,
> And see that the day has dawned;
> Now the little birds are singing,
> And the moon has set.

Spanish version:

Éstas son las mañanitas
Que cantaba el Rey David.
Hoy por ser día de tu santo,
Te las cantamos a ti.

> *Coro*
> Despierta, mi bien, despierta,
> Mira que ya amaneció;
> Ya los pajaritos cantan,
> La luna ya se metió.

After Mass, everyone returns home for a day of feasting and celebration. Mexican food is known and enjoyed all over the Americas. It is easy to put together some family favorites and some new dishes for a fiesta in honor of Our Lady of Guadalupe.

Decorate the table with red, green, and white (the colors of the Mexican flag), and a centerpiece of dahlias (Mexico's national flower).

---

* Or saint's day.

MENU

Soup (*optional*)
Refried Beans
Chicken with Mole
Rice
Salad with Mint, Watercress, and Parsley
Flan
Mexican Hot Chocolate

Refried Beans

Homemade refried beans are much better than canned and almost as easy.

Ingredients

1 pound dry pinto or kidney beans, rinsed
2 tablespoons minced garlic
1 medium tomato, diced (fresh or canned)
2 tablespoons ground cumin
1 tablespoon chili powder
1 onion, finely chopped
2 tablespoons bacon fat, shortening, or vegetable oil
salt and pepper to taste

Directions

Place the beans in a large saucepan, and cover with an inch of water. Place over high heat, and bring to a boil. Turn off the heat, and allow the beans to sit for one hour.

After an hour, drain the beans, and cover them with fresh water. Stir in 1 tablespoon of garlic, the tomato, cumin, and chili powder. Bring to a boil over high heat, reduce heat to low, and simmer until the beans are very soft, about 1½ hours, adding water as needed. Once the beans have cooked, remove and mash half.

Heat the bacon fat, shortening, or oil in a large frying pan or skillet, and add the onion. Cook until translucent but not soft.

Add the whole and the mashed beans, along with the remaining tablespoon of garlic, and salt to taste. Add more chili powder if desired. Cook the beans, stirring often, scraping the bottom of the pan as necessary, until they are heated through. Add additional water as needed to achieve the desired consistency.

Serve hot. Serves 4 to 8.

Chicken with Mole

The Spanish word *mole* (pron. *mow-lay*) comes from an Indian word meaning "concoction". Stories about its origins vary, but all suggest that, when an important guest arrived unexpectedly, the cook desperately combined several ingredients to liven up a meal of humble chicken. The results were an instant success.

Children are always thrilled with *mole*. After all, how often are they allowed to eat chocolate for dinner?

Ingredients

¼ cup vegetable oil
4 onions, finely chopped
2 pounds tomatoes, chopped; or one 28-ounce can of chopped tomatoes with the juice
4 hot chile peppers, minced; or 2–4 tablespoons of dried chili flakes
2 tablespoons finely chopped fresh cilantro
ground black pepper to taste
1 teaspoon white sugar
6 skinless, boneless chicken breast halves; or six chicken legs separated into thighs and drumsticks; or a roasting chicken cut into pieces
½ cup chopped fresh oregano
1 teaspoon ground cinnamon
2 teaspoons ground cumin
2 bay leaves
4 squares (1 ounce each) unsweetened chocolate, grated
juice of 1 lime
¼ cup chopped fresh parsley or cilantro (for garnish)
4–6 cups cooked rice

Directions

Heat the oil in a large deep skillet over medium heat. Add the chopped onions, and cook for a few minutes; then stir in the tomatoes, and cook for a few minutes until they release all their juice.

Stir in the hot chile peppers, cilantro, black pepper, and sugar. Bring to a boil, and let it cook for about 10 minutes to thicken.

Add the chicken to the skillet, along with the oregano, cinnamon, cumin, bay leaves, chocolate, and lime juice. Stir to blend all the ingredients, and simmer over medium heat for 15 to 30 minutes—or until chicken pieces are cooked through.

Remove bay leaves, and serve chicken smothered in sauce over rice. Garnish with additional fresh parsley or cilantro.

Serves 6 to 8.

Salad with Mint, Watercress, and Parsley

Ingredients

¾ cup olive oil
3 tablespoons fresh lemon juice
salt to taste
½ teaspoon freshly ground pepper or to taste
1 clove garlic, minced (optional)
1 small head romaine lettuce, washed and torn into small pieces
1 small head red lettuce, washed and torn into small pieces
1 bunch fresh flat-leaf (Italian) parsley, stems removed
1 bunch fresh mint, stems removed
2 watercress, stems removed

Directions

Combine the oil, lemon juice, garlic, salt, and pepper in a small bowl. Whisk to dissolve the salt and form a dressing.

In a salad bowl, combine the romaine, red lettuce, parsley, mint, and watercress. Drizzle the dressing over the greens, and toss to coat evenly. Serve immediately.

Mexican Hot Chocolate

Ingredients

¼ cup unsweetened cocoa (not hot-chocolate mix!)
¼ cup white sugar
¾ teaspoon ground cinnamon (or more to taste)
pinch of salt (to taste)
4 cups milk
½ cup half-and-half cream (10 to 15 percent butterfat)
¾ teaspoon vanilla extract

Directions

In a small bowl or large measuring cup, combine the cocoa, sugar, cinnamon, and salt.

Heat 1 cup of milk in a saucepan until just beginning to bubble—watch it closely (milk will boil over when it reaches boiling point). Remove from heat.

Slowly add the hot milk to the cocoa mixture, whisking until smooth. Return the chocolate milk mixture to the saucepan, and place it over the heat again. Allow it to come to a boil over low heat. Stir in the remaining 3 cups of milk, and return to boiling.

Before serving, whisk until frothy, stir in the cream and vanilla. Serve hot. Serves 4 to 6.

Piñatas

Piñatas are a traditional Mexican decoration and party game.

Instructions for making a piñata are given in *Advent, Christmas and Epiphany in the Domestic Church* (Ignatius Press, 2001).

Crafts

Nebraska; Louisiana; Luxembourg; Maine; Mariners; Maryland; Massachusetts; Merizo, Guam; Mexico; Archdiocese of Miami, Florida; Michigan; Minnesota; Mississippi; Missouri;

Making Rosaries

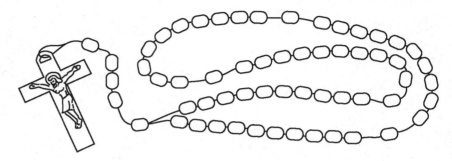

The Rosary is perhaps the most popular of all Catholic devotions. It is a beautiful expression of faith, an effective practice, and a discipline of prayer. Our Blessed Mother told the three children of Fatima, Portugal, in 1917 that, among other things, the peace of the world and the salvation of souls depended upon praying the Rosary. "Otherwise," she said, "the evils of Russia will surround the world."

While it is possible to pray the Rosary on your fingers, a well-made, attractive rosary is a definite improvement. A well-made rosary is one that slides through your fingers smoothly and easily, has easily distinguished spaces between the Hail Mary beads and the Our Father beads, is sturdy enough to carry in a pocket or hang from a hook, and heavy enough to feel while still light enough to carry easily. A well-made rosary can be made of beads on wire, of beads on cord, or of knotted cord.

The first time I attempted to make a bead and wire rosary, it took me about an hour to learn the techniques and then about ten hours to complete the rosary. With practice, the time has decreased to about five hours to complete one. You can make a beautiful rosary in a few evenings or afternoons.

A rosary you've made yourself makes a wonderful gift. Once you've mastered making loops and bows, you can make matching rosaries as wedding presents—an inexpensive, easily mailed gift for a Catholic couple—and for First Communion and Confirmation gifts.

In addition to making rosaries, learning the techniques will help you repair old rosaries. These beautiful treasures of our mother's and grandmother's day should not be forgotten in an old jewelry box or discarded. They should be rescued, restored, and handed down to our children and grandchildren.

Some people make rosaries for missions and missionaries. This is a great gift of time, effort, and prayer. A person will treasure a beautiful hand-made rosary received from a friend or a loved one. We all treasure a rosary we make

ourselves. In no small way, these rosaries can bring us closer to the loving arms of Mary. So, why not try making one yourself?

Cord rosaries (consisting of "beads" made from special knots, or beads strung on cord and separated by knots) are also enjoyable to make. They are a lot faster and less expensive to make than wire rosaries: one or two could easily be made in an afternoon. Large "family" rosaries are usually made this way.

Children can quickly master the skills for making cord rosaries. In many ways, the small, nimble fingers of children are better suited to this craft than those of an adult. The skill is especially suited to girls, who tend to be better at concentrating on such things.

Beads, wire, and special jewelry- or rosary-pliers can be purchased at a craft or bead store, and crucifixes and other supplies can be purchased from rosary-supply companies. Here are a few companies that offer catalogues and free instruction booklets:

Lewis and Company
391 Third Avenue
P.O. Box 268
Troy, New York 12181
Phone: 518-235-1700
Fax: 518-235-0786
URL: http://www.rosaryparts.com

Our Lady's Rosary Makers
4611 Poplar Level Road
P.O. Box 37080
Louisville, Kentucky 40233
Phone: 502-968-1434
Fax: 502-969-8883

The Rosary Shop
2278 N.W. Mahala Way
McMinnville, Oregon 97128
Phone: 503-472-4727
Fax: 503-472-7937
URL: http://www.rosaryshop.com

My own directions for wire and cord rosaries follow. Borrowing from the directions provided by the listed rosary companies, I have developed a few shortcuts and hints. The directions may seem complicated when you are reading them; but once you get started, the making of both kinds of rosaries is quite simple and straightforward.

The best hint of all is to practice making a few bead loops or knots before you start making a whole rosary.

Wire Rosaries

Materials

62 beads—this includes a few extras. If you are using different-size beads for the Our Fathers and the Hail Marys, you will need 55 small beads, and 7 large beads.

8 feet of wire—enough to make one rosary (with a few mistakes). Choices include: aluminum (aluminium) wire; nickel-silver wire; sterling-silver, silver-filled, or gold-filled wire.

crucifix—with a loop at the top

center piece—with three loops

rosary pliers (or jewelry pliers)—small needle-nosed type

wire-cutting pliers (rosary pliers include this function)

Directions

Making a Loop

1. Cut a length of wire that you can comfortably hold and manipulate (about 6 to 8 inches). Hold the wire in one hand so that the natural curve of the wire follows the curve of your palm.

2. Grip the very end of the wire with the pliers, so that none of the end of the wire sticks out. The size of the wire loop is determined by how far up on the pliers' tapered tines the wire is placed.

3. Turn the pliers while holding the wire snugly against the pliers with your free thumb and forefinger, until the wire has made a complete circle. (Using both hands to make the loop will help keep your hands and wrists from getting tired.) You will have a shape like a shepherd's crook.

4. Keeping the tine of the pliers inside the loop, loosen your grip slightly, and rotate the pliers clockwise as far as they will go. Again tighten your grip, and continue bending the wire as before, until you have a nearly closed loop.

5. Remove the pliers from the loop, and then close it completely by placing the tines of the pliers on the outside of the loop, as shown by the black circles in the illustration. Pinch the loop together carefully and gently. Try to keep it circular rather than squeezing it into an oval. It's fine if it remains slightly open.

Making a Bead-Link

6. Thread a bead onto the wire and move it up to your loop. Place the tips of the pliers snugly up against the bead, with the wire about as far up on the tines of the pliers as for the first loop, so that the next loop will be the same size as the first.

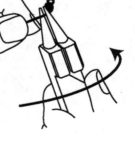

7. Again, rotate the pliers as before to form a U-shape loop.

8. Cut the wire so that the end is even with the bead, as shown below.

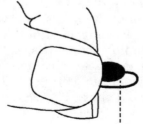

9. Carefully pinch closed the new loop, so that the end of the wire meets the beginning of the loop. The bead should not be too loose but should rotate freely on the wire.

You have made the first bead link.

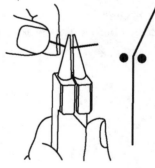

10. Set the first bead-link aside, and repeat steps 6 through 9 to form the next one. This time, before closing the second loop of the link completely, hook it through the last closed loop of your first bead-link, and then close it. Continue making bead links and connecting them until you have a group of ten beads.

Making a Bow-Link

Though it takes some practice to make even bow-links, they are attractive and extremely strong. Strength is appreciated in a homemade rosary.

11. Holding the pliers in one hand and the wire in the other, grasp the wire with the pliers about ¼ inch from the end. Bend the wire to a 45-degree angle where it meets the pliers.

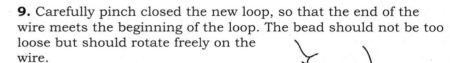

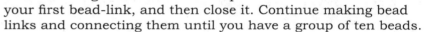

12. Move the pliers to grip the wire on the long side of the angle you've just made. Rotate the pliers to make a full-circle loop, as you did when making the bead-links, so that it now looks like this:

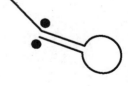

13. Next, rotate the pliers inside the loop until the tine outside the loop is against the ¼-inch stub of wire. Bend the long end of wire until it runs parallel to the stub.

14. Make a 45-degree angle in the long wire, as before, and make another next to this angle. Your bow-link will now look like a long figure-8.

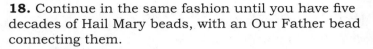

15. Slip the end of your first decade chain onto the first loop of the bow-link. (You will attach the first bead loop of the next decade chain onto the other end of the bow by hooking the new loop through the closed loop of the bow-link.)

16. To complete the bow-link, grip your second loop with the pliers and wrap the long end of wire snugly around the two center wires, as shown at right, from one loop to the other. Cut off the remaining wire and pinch the cut end back into the wrapped coil. You have completed the bow, and your first decade of Hail Mary beads is attached to your first bow-link.

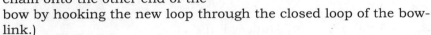

17. Use the directions for making a bead-link to add an Our Father bead to the free side of the bow-link. Make another bow-link to attach to the free side of the Our Father bead.

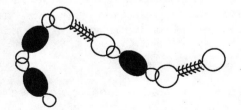

18. Continue in the same fashion until you have five decades of Hail Mary beads, with an Our Father bead connecting them.

Then make the section consisting of an Our Father bead, three Hail Mary beads, another Our Father bead, and the crucifix, as shown below.

Completing the Rosary

19. Note that the center piece you are using may be so shaped as to have a "top" and a "bottom". The string of five decades attaches to the top, and the section with the crucifix and the five beads attaches to the bottom, using bow-links, as shown in the diagram.

Wind off these last connecting bow-links only after all parts are attached.

20. Examine your rosary carefully. Run it through your fingers. If you feel any sharp wires sticking out, crimp them back.

Congratulations! You have completed your first wire rosary!

Making Knotted-Cord Rosaries

Knotted rosaries are simple, inexpensive, and easy even for a child to make. They can be made anywhere (because there are no small pieces to drop), so, besides making them at home as a craft activity, this is a suitable project for a car trip or while at a hotel or cottage. They are also very tough and will last a long time.

Knotted-cord rosaries use a single special knot as beads and closings. When finished, the knot looks like a little seed or nut, made with just three or four tight wrappings of cord around the main cord.

Once you have done one knot, the process will all make sense, and you'll be surprised how easily you can make and place the knots.

Children from age eight should be able to make a knotted-cord rosary. Younger children will need some help at first and might have difficulty keeping their knots perfectly spaced. If your younger child is a perfectionist, he may find this craft a bit frustrating at first.

Materials

Nylon cord or twine. (Nylon cord will not stretch or fray as much as cotton cord. It comes in different thicknesses, sized by number as multiples of 12.)

 #36 twine - 6 yards
 #48 twine - 7 yards
 #60 twine - 9 yards
 #72 twine - 10 yards
 #96 twine - 12 yards

Your finger (or a blunt pencil)
Scissors
Cigarette lighter or matches. (An adult should use these to melt the end of the cord to keep it from unraveling. Be careful: the melted end will be very hot for a few seconds.)

Directions

Hail Mary Knots

1. Drape the cord about 10 inches from one end over your left "pointer" finger or over a pencil held in your left hand, and hold it in place with your thumb. The free end will be held against your left palm with your other fingers.

2. With the remaining cord held in your right hand, loosely wrap it clockwise (away from you) around the cord and your finger. Make three wraps around your finger or the pencil, with each wrap closer to your hand.

3. Then push the cord under all the wraps and pull the entire length through. Slide the loose knot off your finger or pencil and tighten it. The nylon cord slides very easily, and the knot is quite easy to tighten (this is especially helpful when placing the rest of your knots). This is your first Hail Mary knot.

4. Make another knot in the same way, with your first knot held against your left pointer finger (or the pencil) with your thumb. When you slide the second knot off, move the loose knot along the cord until it is close to, but not touching, the first knot. Then, as you tighten your second knot by drawing the cord through, maneuver it a short distance away from the first knot.

To maneuver the knot, hold the cord and existing knots with your left hand, and simultaneously roll and nudge the new knot into position with your right thumb and pointer finger while pulling on the free end of the twine with your remaining right-hand fingers.

Our Father Knots

5. An Our Father knot is made the same way as a Hail Mary knot, but the cord is wrapped around six times, to make a larger knot. In addition, when you slide the loose Our Father knot off your finger, remember while you're tightening it to leave a larger space between it and the last Hail Mary knot.

The Rosary Body

Once you have practiced making some Hail Mary knots and some Our Father knots, begin with a full length of twine, leaving about 10 inches of cord at the start before you form your first Hail Mary knot. Then proceed to tie your first decade of knots, then a spaced Our Father knot, then the second decade, and so on, till you have five decades.

At this point, you should have a section of unused twine at both ends.

The Rosary "Tail"

Join the two ends of your work in this fashion, to form the "tail".

1. Holding both the first Hail Mary and the last Hail Mary against your left "pointer" finger with your thumb, wrap the two end cords around your finger clockwise three times. One cord is ten inches, the other is longer.

2. As with the other knots, push the ends of the pair of cords through the loose windings on your finger; and pull the entire length through. (You might need to push each piece of cord through separately. Start with the shorter cord, and do not take the knot off your finger until you have both cords through.) The result will be a knot the same size as the other Our Father knots.

3. Leaving the shorter length of cord free, use the longer cord to do the following:

—make one Our Father knot; leave a space

—make three Hail Mary knots; leave a space

—and make a final Our Father knot.

4. Burn off (do not cut, it will fray too much) the shorter cord remaining at the joining knot. Because the melted cord remains very hot for a few seconds, this should be done by an adult. Save this shorter length to use for the cross-bar of the cross.

The Rosary Cross

Examine the diagram and follow these steps:

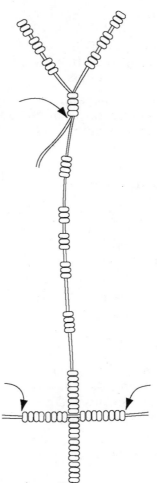

1. Leave a space (the same space between Our Father knots and Hail Mary knots) from the last completed Our Father knot, and make the first knot that will form the cross. Then make four or five more such knots spaced very closely together.*

2. To make the cross-bar, take the piece of cord you just burned off, and place it flat on your lap or a table. On top of it position the vertical row of knots, so that the cord underneath is between the second and third knots. Tie the small cord tightly between those two knots, and then tie two Our Father knots, closely spaced, in the two "arms" of the cross. Finally, check that all knots are very tight, and burn off the ends of the cross-bar.

* If you prefer a smaller cross, reduce the number of knots: e.g., use 3 or 4 knots for the upright, and 2 knots for the cross-bar.

Bead-and-Cord Rosaries

Bead-and-cord rosaries are also very inexpensive, strong, and easy to make. Children can make them quite easily. In fact, if you have a patient child who is between the ages of eight and fourteen, a younger child (ages three to seven) could help by threading the beads while the older child ties the knots.

Because the materials and directions are so simple, and the rosary is finished quite quickly, bead-and-cord rosaries are also good projects to do while at a cottage or summer camp.

Materials
63 beads of your choice. (This includes extra, in case you lose a few. If you are using different-sized beads, you will need 55 small beads, 7 large beads, and 1 larger bead with a hole big enough for two thicknesses of cord.)
8 feet of nylon cord (enough to make one rosary—and some mistakes)
A plastic or metal crucifix
Clear nail polish or shellac
Pair of sharp scissors

Directions

1. Dip both ends of the cord into nail polish or shellac. The stiffened end will make it easier to thread the beads. Allow the cord ends to dry; this might take half an hour or more. (To save time, you could cut and prepare several cord-lengths at once, if you are making more than one rosary.)

2. Measure 8 inches from one end of the cord. Make the first knot here.

The knots are constructed the same way as for knotted-cord rosaries, but each knot is wrapped only twice instead of three or six times.

3. Thread a bead onto the long end of the cord, and slide it up against your first knot.

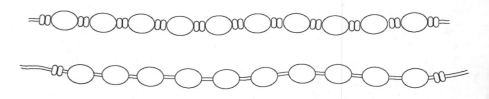

Now you have a choice. Each bead can be held in place between knots (as shown below, top), or each decade can be threaded as a group and be held in place, and be separated from the Our Father beads, by knots (as shown below, bottom).

For either type of decade, thread the bead or beads, then form a second knot—remembering to wrap only twice, then sliding the knot off your finger and tightening.

4. If you are making your rosary with each bead separated by a knot, maneuver the knot close to the bead as you are tightening it. There should be a very small space between the beads and knots to allow the beads to turn freely as they move through your fingers when you are praying. This spacing will also make it easier to fold the rosary up to carry in a pouch or pocket.

If you are making your rosary with each decade strung between end-knots only, place the closing knot a short distance from the last bead, so that the beads can move freely within the decade.

5. Now place an Our Father bead on the cord:

First form a knot to hold the Our Father bead in place, leaving a space of about a finger's width (though this will depend somewhat on the size of your beads) between it and the last knot of the decade.

Then thread a bead and tie a knot, tightening it snugly, but not tightly, up against the bead. You can use a larger bead for the Our Father beads, or all beads of the same size. Usually the different spacing is enough to be able to distinguish them.

6. Continue stringing beads and tying knots until you have five decades made.

7. Hold the first Hail Mary bead of the first decade and the last Hail Mary bead of the last decade together in your left hand with the ends of the cords lying across your pointer finger. Make a knot, but this time wrap the cord around your finger only once. Leave the same space between the Hail Mary beads and this knot as you have left for the Our Father beads.

8. String the largest bead onto both cords, and tie another knot to hold it in place.

9. Burn off *one* of the cords close to this last knot with a match or lighter. An adult should do this.

10. Make the "tail" of the rosary in the same way you made the decades, but stringing only three Hail Mary beads instead of ten.

11. The cross can be made in three ways:

• Tie a plastic crucifix onto the end of the "tail".

• Make a knotted crucifix as described in the section for Knotted-Cord Rosaries (page 57).

• Make a crucifix with beads and knots by stringing five beads onto the cord and holding them in place with a knot. Burn the remaining cord off with a lighter or match. Tie a short piece of cord between the second and third beads (as described in the section about Knotted-Cord Rosaries—page 57), and string two beads onto each end. Hold them in place with a knot, and burn off the tips of the cord.

Birthstone Rosaries

A rosary made with someone's birthstone (or semi-precious or costume beads) makes a touching gift. A rosary made with the birthstones of her children will be a mother's treasure.

January	Garnet (deep wine-red)
February	Amethyst (pale purple)
March	Aquamarine, Bloodstone (light blue)
April	Diamond, Crystal, Mother of Pearl (clear)
May	Emerald, Green Onyx (green)
June	Alexandrite, Pearl, Moonstone (white)
July	Ruby (red), Jasper (green)
August	Peridot (yellowish-green), Carnelian (deep blood-red)
September	Sapphire, Lapis (deep blue)
October	Opal, Tourmaline (creamy white, flecks of other colors)
November	Topaz, Citrine (tawny yellow)
December	Turquoise (green-blue)

Yachtsmen; Zacatecas, Mexico; Zamboanga City, Philippines. **TITLES OF MARY:** Adam's Deliverance; Advocate of Eve; Advocate of Sinners; All Chaste; All Fair and Immaculate; All

Mary (and Joseph) Cloaks

Shortly after we began reading J. R. R. Tolkien's *Lord of the Rings* aloud to our children—which we have done three times—our boys began playing "Lord of the Rings", leaping and racing around the yard with wooden sticks used as Gandalf-staffs and swords.

I made them cloaks from old bedspreads and watched in amazement as their play became more elaborate with the addition of costumes. Boys need heroes to guide them as they grow into men, and, as it turns out, many of those heroes wore cloaks.

Costume play is essential in developing a child's imagination, and imagination is an important part of learning. Imagination helps us "put ourselves in someone else's shoes", the first step toward developing love and charity toward our neighbor. Imagination helps us behave with honesty, integrity, and faith as we ask ourselves, "What would Mary—or my patron saint—or Saint Joseph do?" A child with a good imagination is not dependent on television or other such entertainments for his play ideas and (eventually) his values.

If we wish our children to play in healthy and constructive ways, we need to provide them with simple and flexible "props" that can become anything the child's imagination needs. A garbage-can lid serves well as Saint George's shield, and a stick or cardboard sword can serve as Saint Michael's sword. Cloaks can be used as costumes for many diverse characters, such as:

Saint Joseph
Robin Hood
Saint Francis
King Arthur
Luke Skywalker
Aragorn (also known as Strider)
Captain Hook
Frodo Baggins
The Virgin Mary
Maid Marian
Princess Leia Organa

Cloaks are simple to make and relatively inexpensive (especially when you consider the play value—my boys are still using the cloaks I made for them eight years ago). Though cloaks can be sewn by hand, a sewing machine makes the project a lot easier.

Materials

Suitable fabric, such as an old twin-size bedspread or other durable material. A dark color works best. A lightweight blanket is another good choice. (I bought bedspreads—not quilts—at a second-hand store for about five dollars each.)
Scissors
A sheet of paper
Chalk, for marking fabric
A large button or an old leather buckle
Braid, ribbon or leather shoelaces
Needle and thread, or sewing machine

Directions

1. Measure the length of the cloak from the back of your child's neck to the desired length. While it's best to make the cloak as long as possible to allow for growth, it should not be longer than the back of your child's heel to avoid his tripping on it. Write this measurement down.

2. Fold the material lengthwise to make a rectangle. The length of the folded material needs to be a little longer than the measurement you just made.

3. On a sheet of paper, draw a circle that will fit comfortably but not too loosely around your child's neck. The neck is not really a circle (it is wider across the shoulders than it is front to back), so the neck hole will have more room at the front and back than it does at the shoulders. Cut out this circle, and fold it in half.

4. Fold the half circle a third of the way along the folded edge (see illustration). This will be your pattern for the neck hole that fits around the child's neck.

5. Place the two-thirds section of the folded circle at the top of the folded material. Pin it in place or mark around it with chalk, and cut it out through both thicknesses of cloth.

6. Next, using the measurement you wrote down for length, measure the desired length of cloak from the newly cut neck hole down along the folded edge of the material. Mark this point, then draw a curved line with chalk across the material to the other edges, as shown. This will be the bottom edge of the cloak.

7. Cut along this line.

8. Have your child try on the cloak. Decide how he wants it to fasten at the top of the neck. Adjust the size of the neck hole as necessary. The two front edges of the cloak can join with a button and loop, just bringing the two edges together, or they can cross over a bit and fasten with a large button or belt buckle.

9. Now hem all the cut edges in whatever manner you choose. A single line of ribbon or braid along all the edges, with a decorative loop every once in a while, looks very "authentic". A loop of the braid can be used as the button loop.

The cloak is done, unless your child wants a hood. And what child, given a choice, would not want a hood on his hermit, pilgrim, hobbit, pirate, or forest elf cloak?

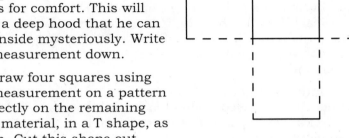

10. To make a hood, measure from your child's shoulder to the top of his head. Add a few inches for comfort. This will make a deep hood that he can hide inside mysteriously. Write this measurement down.

11. Draw four squares using this measurement on a pattern or directly on the remaining cloak material, in a T shape, as shown. Cut this shape out.

Join together the sides drawn with dotted lines, and sew them, to form a boxy hood. Check to see that it fits your child's head, and then sew the hood into the neck hole of the cloak. You will probably have to gather either the hood edge or the cloak edge at the back of the neck to make the two pieces fit nicely.

Sew braid or ribbon onto the front edge of the hood to match the decoration of the cloak. Now the cloak is done.

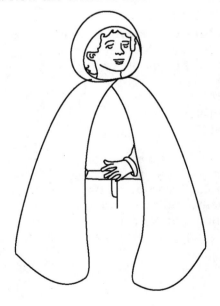

Beeswax Candles for Candlemas

In these times of computers, Internet, holograms, and other technological marvels, what else is as humble yet as compelling as a simple candle? With its steadily burning flame, gently glowing light, and aromatic scent—a lighted candle fascinates and inspires us.

Blessed candles are lit at Mass and other Church services. They are used during the celebration of most sacraments and during other liturgical ceremonies. Every Catholic family should have at least two blessed candles in the home and should use blessed candles when the sacraments are administered to the sick and at times of any special danger, blessing, or family devotion.

Beeswax candles are simple and inexpensive to make by all but the very youngest of children. In addition to their use in your Advent wreath, at your family altar, and for special feasts, homemade beeswax candles make wonderful gifts for friends and relatives.

Materials

Sheets of beeswax (approximately 16 x 8 inches), available from craft stores or Internet stores.
Wick—usually available where you can buy beeswax. (String will not work.)
Hair dryer
Cookie cutters
Waxed paper
Ruler
Sharp knife or good scissors
Empty soup or tomato can
Candle mold(s): can be a purchased mold, or simply an empty cardboard milk container, frozen-juice cylinder, etc.
Ceramic plate, or glass pie dish
Pencil, or chopstick, or skewer

Rolled Candles

Beeswax is easier to handle when warm; work in a warm room if you can. The most important thing to remember is that a loosely rolled candle will burn quickly because more air is available to the flame, so form your candles as tightly as possible.

If the beeswax was rolled when you bought it, gently unroll it. If it is stiff, or if it cracks while unrolling, soften it by gently warming it with a hair dryer set on low.

Lay a length of wick along a shorter edge, and firmly fold the wax over it. Squeeze it together firmly. The wax is slightly sticky, so this step is easier than it sounds. Begin rolling the candle, making sure that it is rolled as tightly and evenly as possible.

When you have finished rolling up the sheet of wax, run the hair dryer over it to mold the edges together, and to soften the bottom so that you can give it a flat, smooth surface.

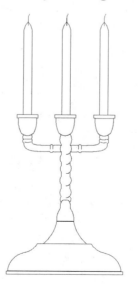
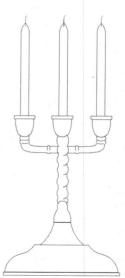

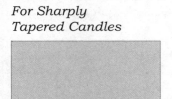

Tapered Candles

The procedure just described will give you a straight, thick candle. If you prefer a tapered candle, cut the sheet of beeswax according to the patterns given. To make sure your cut is straight, use a ruler as a guide.

For Sharply Tapered Candles   *For Gently Tapered Candles*

Because you cut the sheet in half, you will end up with a pair of matched candles. If you wish, you can lay two sheets of different colors, one on top of the other, before you start rolling. This will give you a layered and striped candle.

Flat Candles

This method is especially good for younger children, who might find rolling the wax sheet difficult. There are many variations of shapes and colors possible with this method of candle making.

Begin by unrolling the sheet of beeswax. Select a cookie cutter—such as a star, a circle, or an angel—and cut out an *even* number of shapes from the sheet of wax. Twelve to sixteen pieces is enough.

Divide your pile of shapes in half. Working on a sheet of waxed paper, put one piece on top of another, and press them together, making sure that they are firmly stuck together. (Children enjoy this part.)

When you have "sandwiched" half of your shapes, lay a piece of wick across the top with one end sticking out a little, and continue to press the other wax pieces onto your sandwich, trapping the wick between the two thick layers of wax pieces. If necessary, occasionally heat it with the hair dryer, to help the wax stick together.

When you have finished, peel the candle off the wax paper, trim the wick, and set your candle upright.

Poured Candles

Here is a way to use the left-over pieces of beeswax. Collect the scraps, and melt them in a can set in simmering water. Use a small soup or tomato can rather than a pot, so that you can simply throw the can away when you are finished.

> CAUTION: *Always melt wax in a can placed in simmering water, not directly over the heat! Hot wax can start a fire if it gets too hot or spills into a flame!*

While the wax is melting, prepare a mold for the candle. You could purchase a candle mold when you buy the beeswax, but a mold can also be made of almost any container taller than it is wide. A waxed-cardboard milk container, or a frozen-juice concentrate can, makes a good candle mold.

Tie a knot in a length of wick a little longer than the height of your mold. Poke a very small hole through the bottom of the improvised mold, and thread the wick through it, with the knot on the outside. Tie the other end to a pencil, chopstick, or skewer laid across the top of the mold so that it is held taut. Set your mold on a ceramic plate or glass pie dish. When you pour the wax, pour a small amount in first and let it harden to seal the wick hole.

Pour most of the rest of the melted wax into the mold (reserve some). Let it sit undisturbed until the wax is hardened. Wax shrinks slightly as it cools, and you will need to pour more wax into your mold after about 45 minutes. Poke a skewer or thin knife into the candle along the wick to open up the shrinkage "well". Gently pour more wax into the well. Allow the candle to cool for several hours or overnight.

After the wax is fully set, slip the candle out of the mold, or tear the mold off. Turn the candle over, and untie the knot. This is now the *top* of your candle. Smooth the bottom if necessary to help it stand straight and steady.

Mary Dolls

Children's play (and the imagination that fuels it) is a safe, controlled way to explore many concepts, from the physical laws of nature as they play in the sandbox with buckets and the hose, to the complexities of relationships and the development of virtues and values as they play "cowboys and indians" or "house".

These Mary Dolls are not statues or *objets d'art*. They are meant to be played with and to allow children to place Mary firmly in their imaginations and their hearts. If the dolls end up tattered or topsy-turvy under the bed, it is not disrespect but a sign that the dolls and Mary have been welcomed into their play.

Materials

A doll or dolls—such as purchased or homemade cloth dolls (not baby dolls) or inexpensive plastic dolls

Fabric and trim of various weights in shades of blue, white, and gold. Quilting stores are an excellent source of small amounts of wonderfully patterned cloth—for example, with stars for Our Lady of Guadalupe. Inexpensive fabric and trim can be found at second-hand clothing stores—buy the blouse for the fabric, not the fit.

Basic sewing supplies: scissors, pins, thread, needles

Waxed paper or parchment paper, for pattern

Paper plate (optional)

Stapler

Tape

Sheet of paper

Ribbon (for veil)

Heavy cardboard, chamois, or canvas

Dark shoelaces

Directions

1. If you wish the doll to stand up on its own, make a cone with the paper plate by cutting it from the

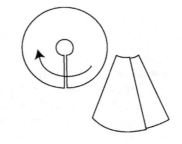

edge to the center. Roll it up into a cone with the desired bottom diameter. Secure the cut edge of the plate with tape. Then cut a hole at the pointed end of the cone just large enough to slip the doll's waist through.

Trim the bottom of the cone so that the doll stands supported by the cone. Remove the cone, and tape the waist and bottom edges to strengthen them; and put extra tape as needed along the cut edge.

2. Decide how you are going to dress Mary.

These directions will dress Mary as Our Lady of Lourdes. Adapt the colors and headdress to your choices.

3. Use this diagram to make a pattern for the dress on the waxed or parchment paper. This dress is not fitted; it is very loose and flowing. Take the following measurements, and adjust your pattern accordingly.

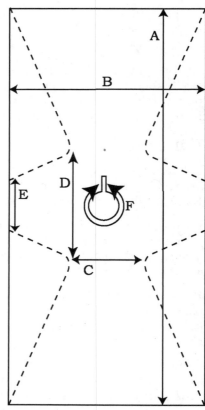

A   Twice the height of the doll, from the shoulders to the feet.

B   From one wrist across the shoulders to the other wrist.

C   Loosely around the doll's chest.

D   Loosely around the doll's armpit.

E   Loosely around the doll's wrist.

F   Loosely around the doll's neck.

4. Cut out a dress piece of white fabric, along the dotted lines.

5. Fold the dress piece in half along the shoulder line, and mark the center.

Cut out the keyhole-shaped neck hole. This needs to be an opening big enough for the doll's head without making the neckline too low. The neck of the dress will fasten with ties at the back.

6. Finish the neckline. This is much easier to do now than when the dress is being sewn together. You can finish this edge very simply by zig-zagging around the opening with a matching or contrasting color thread.

If you like, you could finish the edge by binding it with a piece of ribbon (folding a piece of ribbon over the edge and sewing it in place), extending the ends of the ribbon to make a tie at the back of the neck.

A proper facing is not really worth the effort and probably would not stand up to the rigors of play.

7. Pin the dress, right sides (outsides) together, and sew the arm and body seams. Use a very small seam allowance—¼ inch. Sew this seam twice, then zig-zag over the raw edges.

8. Turn the dress right-side out. Try it on the doll, adjust the length as needed, and then hem it. Mary's dresses are always long, so that her toes or sandals barely show. Hem the doll's dress to this length.

9. Select a piece of blue fabric, and cut out a sash. The sash length should equal the "A" measurement from the dress pattern. The sash width should equal the "E" measurement from the dress pattern. This will make a full, flowing sash that reaches Mary's feet when it has been tied around her waist.

Finish the sash edges. You can finish these edges by zig-zagging them, or by turning the edge under ¼ inch and sewing it, or by binding it with matching ribbon. Tie the sash around the doll's waist.

10. Next, make a veil. At Lourdes, Mary's dress and veil were white. The veil should, if possible, be of a lighter fabric than that of the dress.

On a sheet of paper, draw a circle, using the "A" measurement as the diameter. Cut out this circle. Fold in half, and then cut it on the fold. Using this half-circle as your pattern piece, cut out a veil. Finish the edges of the veil in the same way you finished the sash. (If you were dressing your doll as Our Lady of Guadalupe, the hem of the dress, the sash, and the veil could be trimmed or edge-bound with ornate gold trim.)

11. Drape the veil on the doll's head, with the straight edge on its forehead. To fasten the veil onto the doll's head so that it will stay in place during play, center the veil on the doll's head, measure down on each side to the doll's ears, and mark these points with a pin. Cut a piece of ribbon long enough to tie around the doll's head, like a head-scarf. Sew this ribbon along the edge of the veil, centering it between the two points. Leave the ends free. Place the veil on the doll's head, bring the ends of the ribbon to the back of its head, and tie them.

12. Make sandals for the doll, using either the cardboard, chamois cloth, or canvas. Trace around the doll's foot, and cut out four footprints. Poke eight holes in two *sole* pieces (see drawing). Thread a length of shoelace down through holes 1 and 2, then up through 3 and 4, leaving a loop. Repeat with a second length of shoelace, down through A and B, then up through C and D. Glue a footprint on the bottom of each sole to cover the laces. Attach the sandals to the doll's feet by tying the laces.

Our Lady of Lourdes also carried a rosary. The type of rosary you make for a Mary doll will depend on the size of the doll. A plastic doll for an older girl could have a small and delicate rosary made from seed beads and knotted quilting thread; a soft cloth doll for a younger child might have a knotted-cord rosary. ***Make sure a "play" rosary is too small to fit over a child's head.***

Paper Flowers

Many Marian devotions are better with flowers! Certainly, a statue or icon of Mary on a prayer table or top shelf of the living room bookcase should have flowers with it.

Fresh flowers are not always in season or accessible. Paper flowers are very easy and satisfying to make. A child can make paper flowers without difficulty, and with results good enough that he will feel proud of his accomplishment.

Basic Layered Paper Flowers

This method produces the best-looking flowers, I think.

Materials

Tissue paper (6 sheets or more)
Pencil
Scissors
Green pipe cleaners (also known as chenille stems)

Directions

1. Cut at least six sheets of tissue paper into squares, and lay them on top of each other. The size of the squares will determine the final size of the flower. Squares between 4 and 6 inches are best.

Fold the squares in half, then into quarters.

Fold the resulting square in half diagonally, so that it forms a right triangle.

2. Give this triangle a classic "ice-cream cone" shape by cutting a curved top on the triangle. Unfold and smooth the flower pieces.

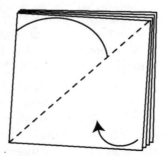

3. With the point of a pencil, carefully poke two small holes near the center of the flower layers.

4. Fold a pipe cleaner in the middle. Thread the ends of the pipe cleaner through the two holes in the layers of tissue paper. Twist the free ends together to form the stem.

5. Pull each sheet of tissue paper upward to form the petals of the "flower", crinkling and bunching them so that they stay upright. When you have pulled up all the sheets, fluff and even out the petals.

Variations

For very simple flowers, after cutting the tissue paper into squares, layer the squares to make an eight-pointed star. Then follow steps 3 through 5, above.

— For unusual and colorful flowers, use different kinds of paper, such as wrapping paper, patterned tissue paper, magazine or newspaper pages, or waxed paper.

— Make the petals more elaborate by cutting them out with pinking shears or craft scissors with shaped blades.

— Make sparkly flowers by brushing the edges of a completed flower with white glue, then dipping the flower into a bowl of glitter.

— String several small flowers together as a garland.

MARY'S FLOWERS

Lilies (*Easter lilies, Madonna lilies, and lilies of the valley*). The white color and sweet fragrance of lilies symbolize Mary's purity, humility, and loving obedience to God's will. Lilies also symbolize virginity; hence many saints (Saint Joseph, in particular) are commonly portrayed holding a lily.

Basic Folded Paper Flowers

These are the classic paper flowers that everyone seems to know how to make (but perhaps they don't look quite as good as layered flowers).

Materials

Multicolored tissue, or crepe paper
Green pipe cleaners (also known as chenille stems)
Scissors

Directions

Take four or five sheets of the tissue or crepe paper, and layer them. (If you want multicolored flowers, use a variety of colors.) Cut the tissue paper into 8-inch squares.

Keeping the sheets layered, fold them like an accordion into a thin rectangle. Each fold should be about ½-inch wide.

At the center of the rectangle, cut a small v-shaped notch on both sides (see diagram). Take the end of a pipe cleaner, and twist it around the notch, so that the pipe cleaner is at a 90-degree angle to the folded side of the rectangle.

Gently pull up one layer of tissue into the center. Pull up the remaining layers, one by one. Repeat for the other side of the flower. Once all the layers are pulled up, twist and fluff them in place to look natural.

Variations

• For sturdier long stems, twist two pipe cleaners together. For sturdier short stems, fold the pipe cleaner in half over the folded rectangle of tissue paper. • To change the size of the flowers, cut smaller or larger squares. • For fluffier or thinner flowers, vary the number of layers of tissue paper. Add more layers for thicker flowers, fewer layers for thinner ones.

Roses

Paper roses are more difficult to make than the basic flowers, but they are beautiful when done.

Materials

Multicolored crepe paper
Green pipe cleaners (also known as chenille stems)
Scissors
Glue
Tape

Directions

1. Form a small ball of tissue paper over the end of a pipe cleaner, wrapping the pipe cleaner around the bottom of the ball and taping or gluing it in place.

2. Cut out at least 10 petals in the shape shown. Stretch each slightly in the direction of the arrow.

3. Glue 6 or 7 petals together as shown below.

4. Place the pipe cleaner and ball on the bottom of these petals, and roll the petals up. You may have to scrunch and fold them slightly to give the rose a bud shape. Glue them in place.

5. You now have a rosebud. To leave it as is, cut 3 or 5 small green leaves (use the same pattern as for the petals), and glue them around the bottom of the bud.

6. To make a larger rose, add more petals. Overlap the petals. About one-third of each new petal should overlap the last petal. Glue the petals in place as you go.

Finish the rose by wrapping its base with a few leaves, the same size as those used for a rosebud. Add a few larger leaves to the stem, if you wish.

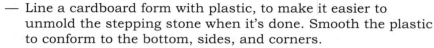
Stepping Stones

Stepping stones or garden markers through your Mary Garden will last for years. The stepping stones can be decorated by pressing patterns of stones, marbles, shells, or bits of colored glass (sharp-side down!) into the wet cement, or by drawing pictures and messages into the wet cement.

Materials

A "form" for your stepping stone. Make a form by nailing pieces of 3-inch wood together, or use existing forms—such as a plastic plant saucer, a sturdy cardboard box, or an old cake pan. Stepping-stone molds are also available for purchase.
Large plastic garbage bag (to line the form)
Ready-mix cement mix
Wire coat hangers (2 or 3)
Wheelbarrow, or large bucket, to mix cement
Water and a hose with sprayer, or a spray bottle of water
Shovel or trowel, to mix cement and scoop it into the form
Decorative items, such as stones, marbles, shells, leaves (to leave a surface impression), bits of colored glass, and special mementos and souvenirs
Popsicle (or similar) stick, to draw designs

Directions

1. Prepare a work area, outdoors; use a heavy plastic dropcloth if you're working on your picnic table. Have clean water ready nearby to wash your hands and tools when you've finished. Avoid leaving wet cement on bare skin for any length of time— it's not instantly dangerous, but it will cause a mild chemical burn if left for more than an hour.

2. Prepare the form:
— Wet a wooden form well. The grain of a wooden form set on a sheet of plywood will leave its impression on the sides and bottom of the finished stepping stone. You could also use a plastic liner inside the wooden form.

— Line a cardboard form with plastic, to make it easier to unmold the stepping stone when it's done. Smooth the plastic to conform to the bottom, sides, and corners.
— A plastic form needs no special preparation.

3. Mix the cement. Measure about twice the volume of your form in cement mix into the mixing bucket or wheelbarrow. Gradually add small amounts of water, and mix well with a stick, trowel, hoe, or shovel until the mixture is wet and pliable, not soupy.

4. "Plop" trowelfuls of cement mix into your form until it is half full. Optional: Reinforce your stepping stone by laying two or three metal coat hangers on top of the cement, bending them into shapes that fit in the form without touching the edges.

5. Continue to add cement to the form until it is full. Tap the sides lightly a few times to remove any air bubbles, and smooth off the top with a straight board. Allow to sit and become stiff— about half an hour (less if you're using quick-set cement).

6. Begin embellishing your stepping stone by pressing stones and other objects firmly into the surface of the cement. Place them randomly or in any desired pattern. If an item sinks too far, simply scoop it out, re-smooth the surface, and position the item again. Use a Popsicle stick to scratch letters or designs on the surface. Allow the stone to dry for another half hour.

7. Brush away the loose pieces of cement from the top of the stepping stone, and mist the surface *lightly* with the hose or a spray bottle. (Keeping the surface slightly damp as the cement sets will slow its curing rate and give a stronger result.) Repeat the misting two or three more times, at an hour's interval. (The cement reaches its full strength in about 30 days.)

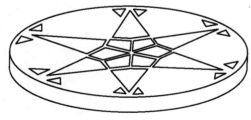

8. Allow the stepping stone to set up overnight, then carefully "pop" it out of the form (or tear away the card-board)—and decide where to place it in your garden!

Mary Baskets

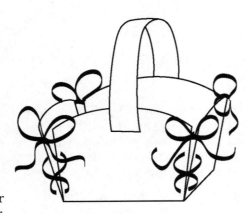

Families use baskets in many ways. In addition to laundry baskets and grocery baskets, we often carry gifts to a friend in a basket, collect Valentine cards in a basket, present Easter eggs in a basket, and arrange flowers in a basket. In our family, we distribute slips of paper with the gifts of the Holy Spirit written on them for Epiphany or Pentecost, or names of family members for an Advent "secret friend", from baskets.

An old May 1 tradition saw homemade paper baskets filled with flowers or treats and left on the doorsteps of friends or neighbors. Though people may look a bit askance at something left on their doorstep today (and it's a shame we live in a time when it is necessary to be wary), the tradition could certainly be modified to allow one to distribute baskets to classmates or relatives.

Children love to make baskets. These "Mary Baskets" are especially cute and easy to make.

Materials

2 decorative paper plates, about 10 inches in diameter
Scrap paper, cut to a 4-inch square
8 feet of ¼-inch wide ribbon, in a color that coordinates with the
    paper plate; cut into 4 even pieces
Scissors
Hole punch
Pencil and ruler
Stapler

Directions

1. Trace the 4-inch square pattern onto the middle of the *bottom* of the decorative plate.

2. Imagine the plate as a tic-tac-toe board, with the 4-inch square as the middle square. Cut out the outside corners of the tic-tac-toe board (along the dotted lines shown on the diagram). This will leave you with a cross shape.

3. Punch out three holes on each of the cut edges of the cross, about ¼ inch from the edge, as shown in the diagram.

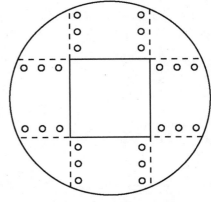

4. Lay the ruler along the fold line (this provides a firm edge to fold against), and fold up the sides of the cross with the decorative side out, to make the sides of the basket. The 4-inch square you traced thus becomes the inside bottom of the basket.

5. Lace the ribbon through the holes, as if lacing a pair of running shoes, and tie it at the top with a pretty bow.

6. Cut a strip across the middle of the second plate about 1½ inches wide. Staple it to the sides of the basket to form the basket's handle. For an extra decorative touch, punch two holes in the middle of the handle, then thread and tie more ribbon through them.

Holding Hands with Mary

I remember this craft from my childhood. How amazed I was when the paper was unfolded to reveal a line of little figures, all holding hands.

This craft is one way to illustrate the mystery of the communion of saints, showing how the baptized faithful form the Mystical Body of Christ. Of course, no such demonstration can ever adequately explain a divine mystery, but, like Saint Patrick's shamrock, this project might help children (and us!) understand the mystery a little better.

Materials

Heavy paper—such as construction paper
    or paper from a large sketch pad
Ruler
Pencil
Scissors
Coloring materials: pencils, crayons
Glue
Ribbon
Scraps of cloth
Yarn

Directions

1. Using the ruler, measure and cut the paper into the shape of a rectangle that is 5 or 6 inches wide and about 30 or 40 inches long.

2. Accordion-fold the paper rectangle, making each fold 3 to 4 inches wide. Trim off any excess after folding.

3. Trace a girl or boy pattern onto the top rectangle of paper, taking care to make sure that the "hands" and "feet" touch the edges, as shown.

4. Cut out the figures, making sure that you *do not cut the hands or feet apart.* Unfold the figures, revealing a row of people, all holding hands.

5. Decorate, making each figure look different.

Variation

Accordion-fold the paper, making each fold about 6 inches wide. (This will work only with very long paper—try to get a roll of craft paper from a craft shop or an end-roll of newsprint from your local newspaper office.)

Trace and cut out the "boy and girl" pattern shown, following steps 3 and 4, above.

Remind the children, while they decorate their rows of people, that even though each looks different—with different hair, faces, and clothing—they all came from the same paper, and they are all still "connected". This is similar to our connection to the Church: we all look different, but we are all God's children, made the same and connected by our love for Jesus.

Memorare Roses—Cross-Stitch Pattern

The Memorare is a beautiful prayer of trust in and devotion to the Queen of Heaven. This cross-stitch prayer does not take long to complete, and it makes a beautiful addition to a child's room.

You can choose whatever colors that you prefer and that complement the color scheme of your home; the chart keys are suggestions only.

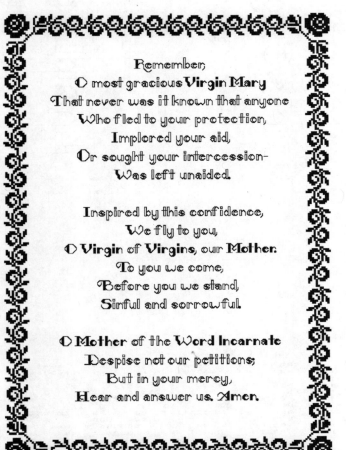

Remember,
O most gracious Virgin Mary
That never was it known that anyone
Who fled to your protection,
Implored your aid,
Or sought your intercession-
Was left unaided.

Inspired by this confidence,
We fly to you,
O Virgin of Virgins, our Mother.
To you we come,
Before you we stand,
Sinful and sorrowful.

O Mother of the Word Incarnate
Despise not our petitions;
But in your mercy,
Hear and answer us. Amen.

How to Do Cross-Stitch

Bring the thread through at the lower right-hand side; insert the needle one block up and one block to the left, and bring out one block down—thus forming a half cross. Continue in this way to the end of the row. Complete the upper half of the cross as shown. Cross-stitch may be worked either from right to left or left to right, but it is important that the upper stroke of all crosses lie in the same direction.

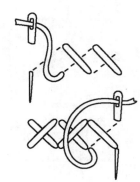

How to Do Running- or Stem-Stitch

Work this stitch to form the lettering of the design. As shown, bring the needle up through one hole of the fabric (1) and down through the second hole along the line of the design (2). Bring the needle back up through the middle hole (3). Continue stitching by inserting the needle two blocks ahead and bringing it up one block back.

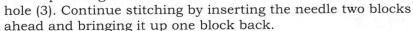

How to Do Back-Stitch

Work this stitch around the cross-stitch letters, if you wish. The method for back-stitch is similar to that for running-stitch. As shown, bring the needle up through one hole of the fabric (1) and down through the first hole away from the direction of your stitching (2). Bring the needle back up two blocks ahead (3). Continue by putting the needle down through your first hole and back up two blocks forward.

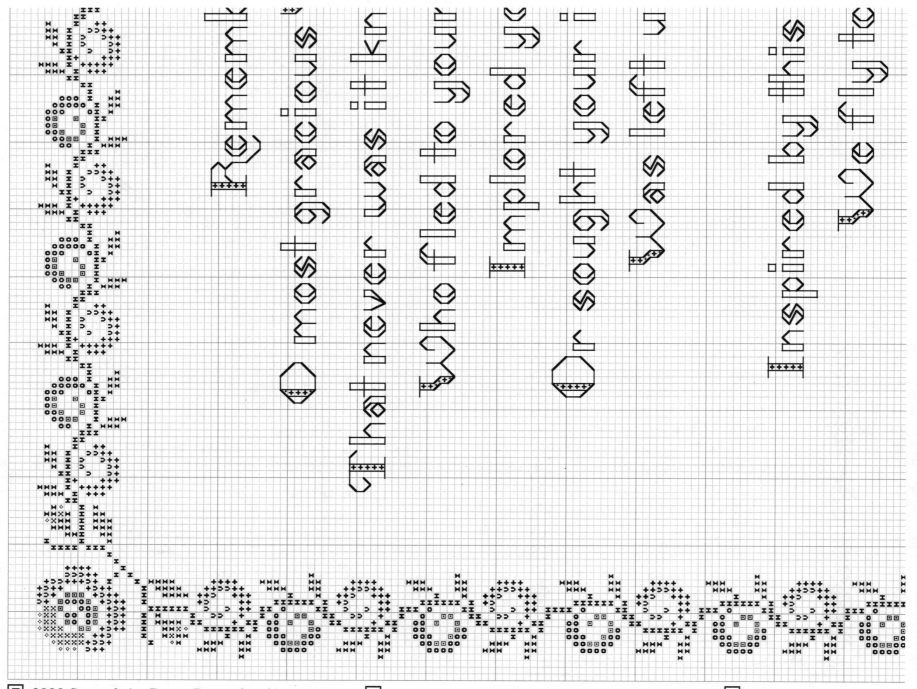

▣ 3822 Straw–lt (or Dusty Rose–ul vy lt)   ◈ 3823 Ultra Pale Yellow (or 819 Baby Pink–lt)   ☒ 701 Christmas Green

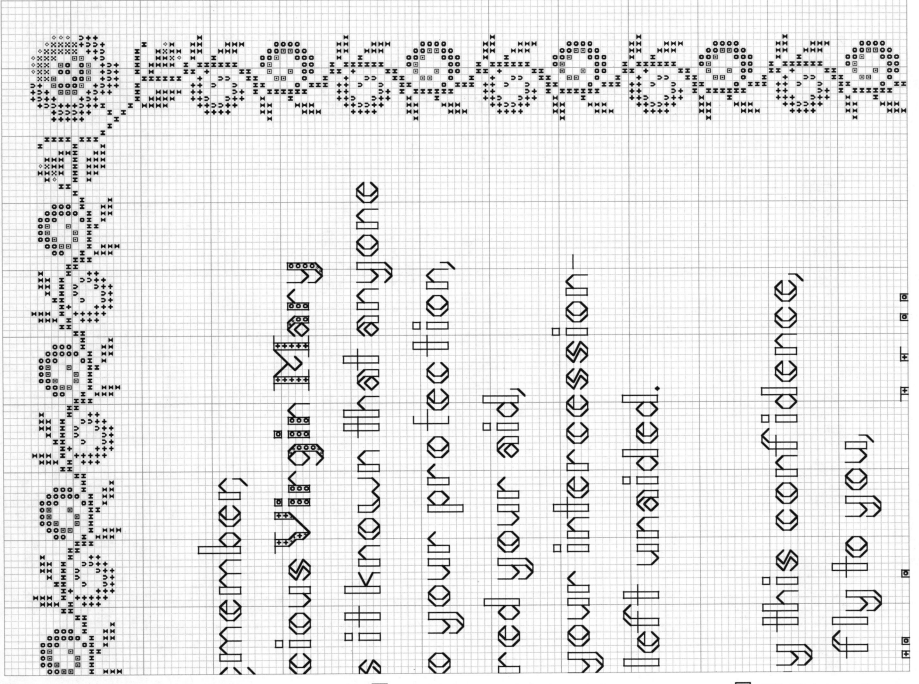

◉ 677 Old Gold–vy lt (or 776 Pink–med) **U** 680 Old Gold–dk (or 309 Rose–deep) **H** 699 Christmas Green

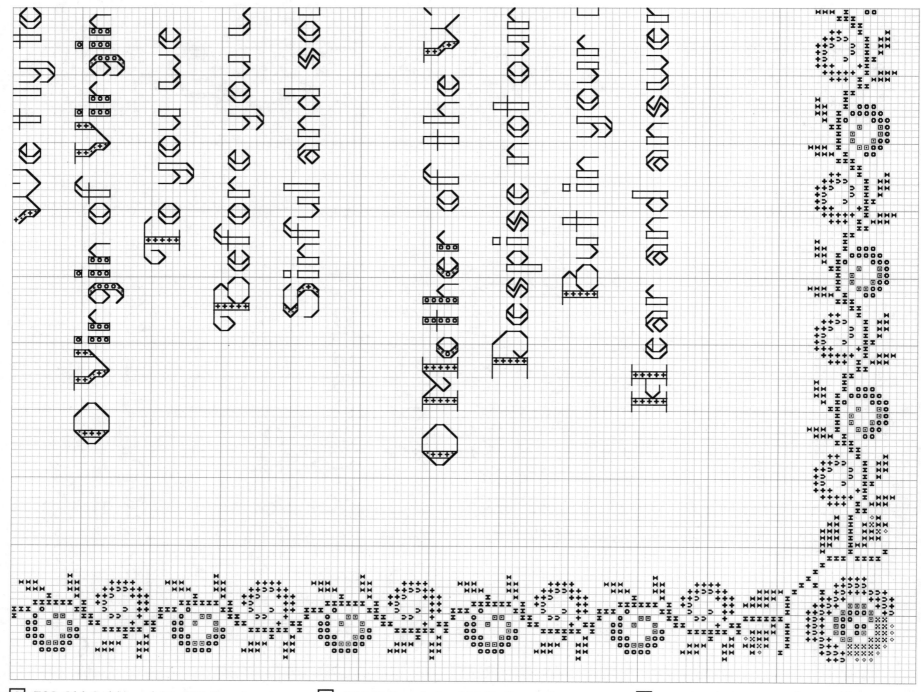

729 Old Gold–med (or 335 Rose) 745 Yellow–lt (or 899 Rose–med) 825 Blue–dk 825 Blue-dk

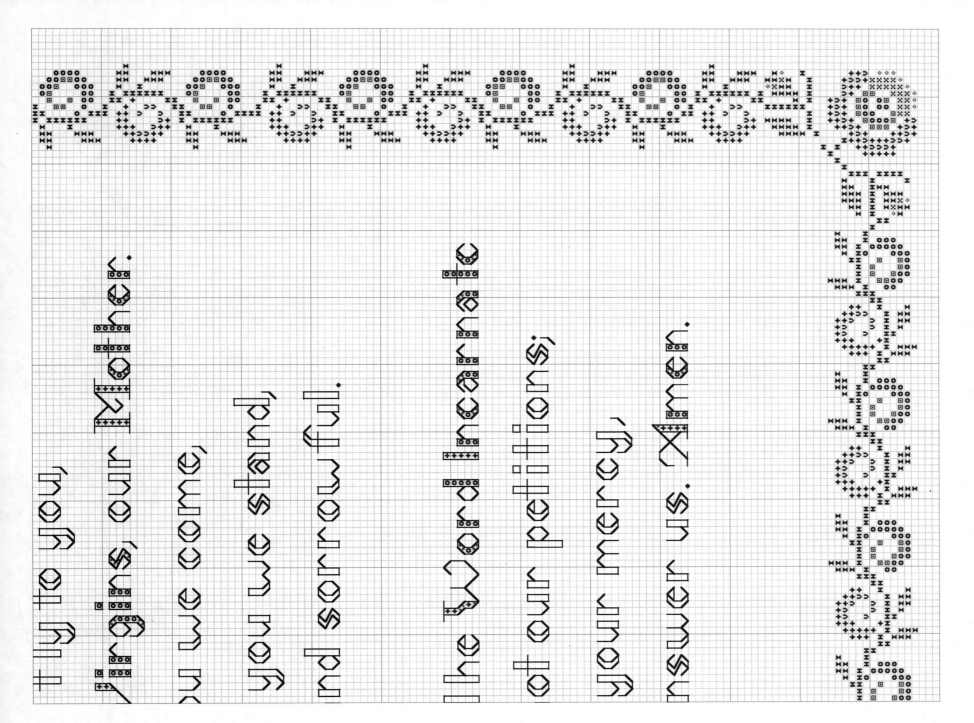

Coloring Pages

Marian Devotions in the Domestic Church: Coloring Pages

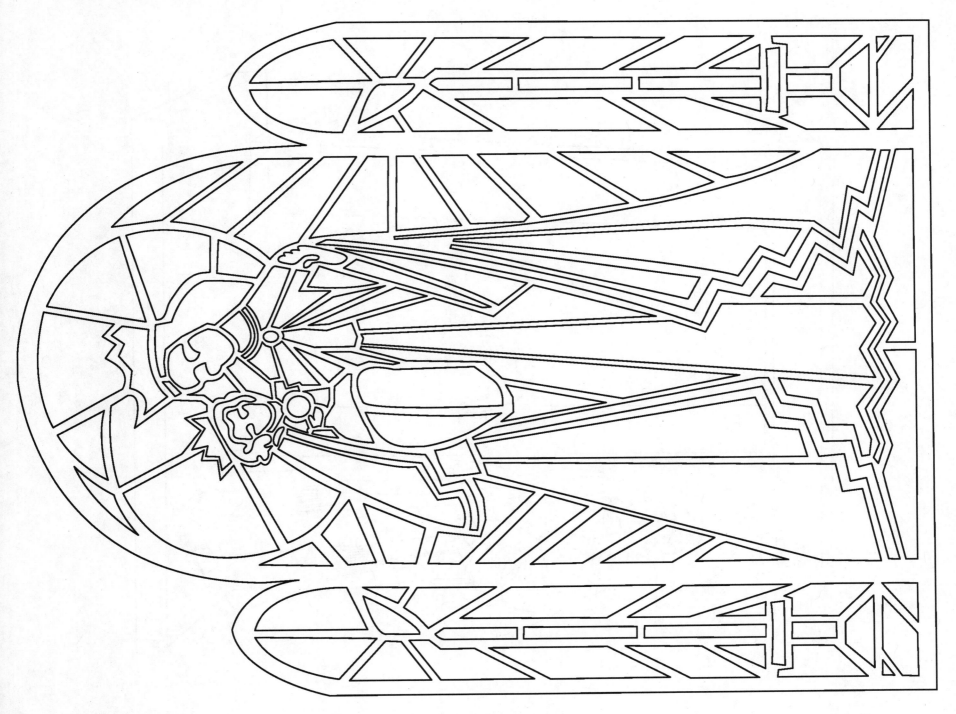

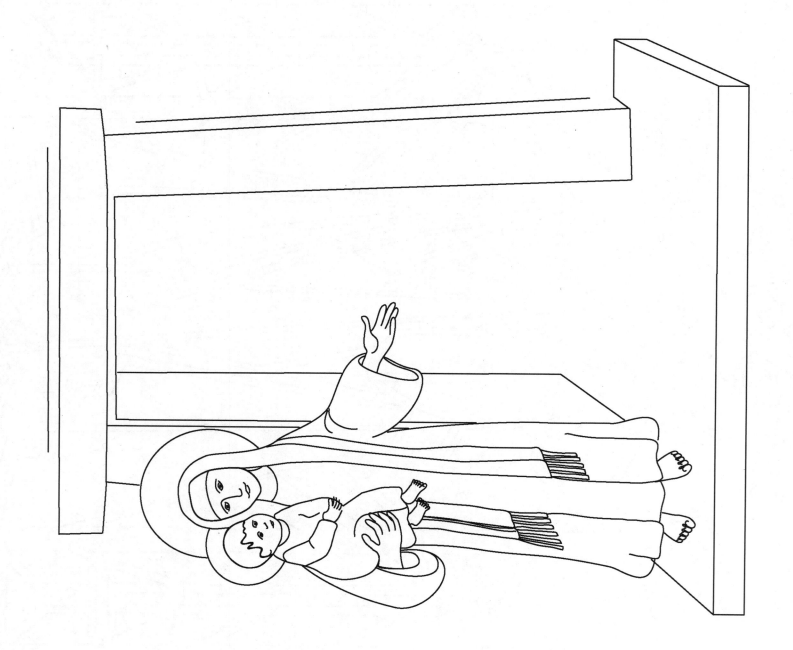

Marian Devotions in the Domestic Church: Coloring Pages

Marian Devotions in the Domestic Church: Coloring Pages www.Domestic-Church.com

Marian Devotions in the Domestic Church: Coloring Pages

Marian Devotions in the Domestic Church: Coloring Pages

Marian Devotions in the Domestic Church: Coloring Pages

Marian Devotions in the Domestic Church: Coloring Pages

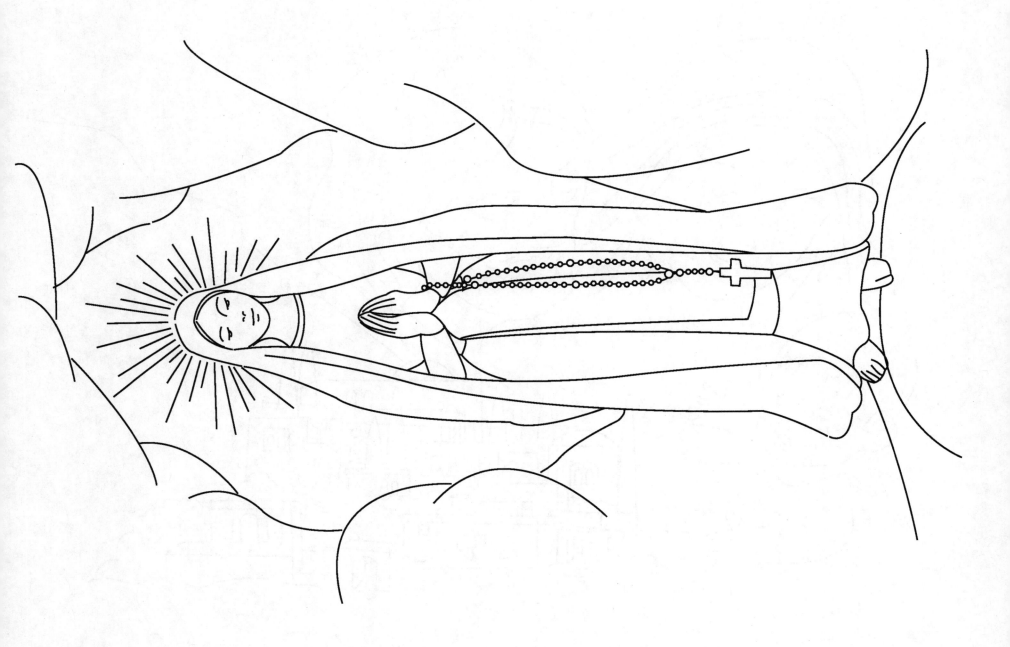

Marian Devotions in the Domestic Church: Coloring Pages

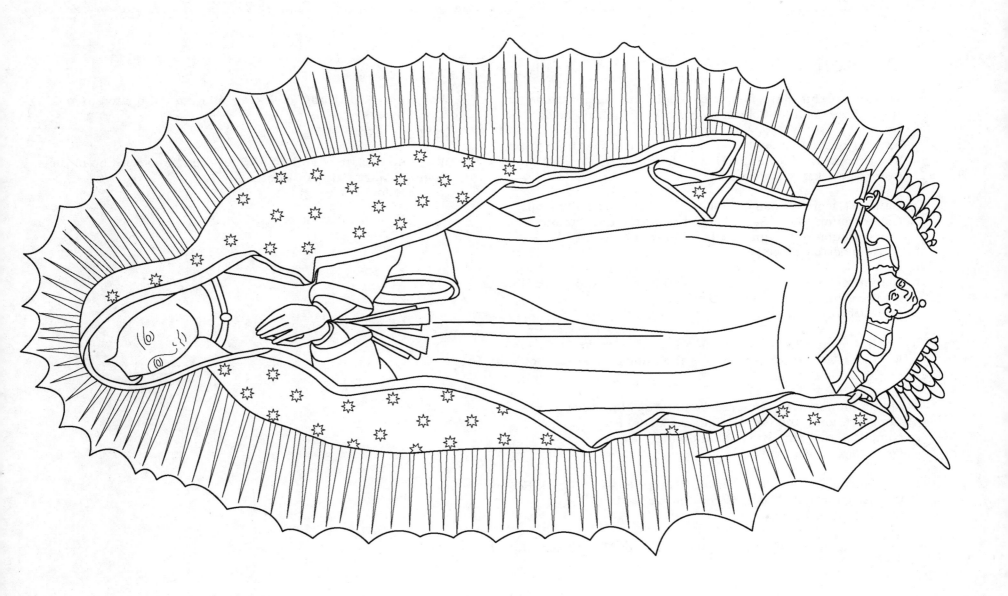

Our Lady of Japan; Our Lady of Kevelaer; Our Lady of Knock; Our Lady of La Leche; Our Lady of La Vang; Our Lady of Las

Acknowledgments

We are grateful to the following people and organizations for their permission to include their materials in this book.

Fathers of the Birmingham Oratory—for extracts from "Mary: The Second Eve", by John Henry Newman.
(www.birmingham-oratory.org.uk)

Catholic Doors Ministry (Saskatoon, Canada)—for "Family Consecration to the Sacred Heart of Jesus" and "Family Consecration to the Immaculate Heart of Mary".
(www.catholicdoors.com)

Communitas Dei Patri and the Family Prayer Night—for "Prayer for the Consecration of the Family".
(www.familyprayernight.org)

Confraternity of Mary Queen of All Hearts Center, Bay Shore, N.Y.—for "Act of Consecration to the Immaculate Heart of Mary", by St. Louis De Montfort.

Militia Immaculata, National Center—for "Prayer of Total Consecration", and for "Miraculous Medal Prayer", both composed by Saint Maximillian Kolbe.
(www.consecration.com)

Dominican Fathers, The Rosary Center (Portland, Ore.), Rosary Confraternity—for "Daily Consecration to Mary".
(www.rosary-center.org)

The estate of Monsignor Thomas Wells—for "The Rosary: A Gift for Our Day".

Women for Faith and Family—for information related to making Mary Flowers.
(www.wf-f.org)

World Apostolate of Fatima (U.S.A.)—for "Consecration of the Home to Mary Help of Christians".
(www.mostholyrosary.org)

Bibliography

Collection of Masses of the Blessed Virgin Mary. Congregation of Divine Worship, 1986.

The Concise Catholic Dictionary. Compiled by Robert C. Broderick. St. Paul, Minn.: Catechetical Guild Educational Society, 1944.

John Paul II. Apostolic Exhortation, *Familiaris Consortio, Regarding the Role of the Christian Family in the Modern World*. Ottawa, Ont.: Canadian Conference of Catholic Bishops, 1984.

———. *Rosarium Virginis Mariae: On the Most Holy Rosary*. Vatican City: 2002. In www.vatican.va.

Paul VI. Apostolic Exhortation, *Marialis Cultis, For the Right Ordering and Development of Devotion to the Blessed Virgin Mary*. Boston, Mass.: Daughters of Saint Paul, 1974.

Pius XII. *Ad Caeli Reginam: On Proclaiming the Queenship of Mary*. Vatican City: 1954. In www.vatican.va.

Resources

Catholic apologetics information: In www.catholicapologetics.info.

Cenacles of the Marian Movement of Priests, Purpose and Guide. St. Francis, Maine: The Marian Movement of Priests, 1999.

De Montfort, Saint Louis-Marie Grignion. *The Secret of Mary*. Adapted by Eddie Doherty. Bay Shore, N.Y.: Montfort Publications, 1962.

———. *True Devotion to Mary*. Translated by Fr. Frederick Faber. Rockford, Ill.: Tan Books and Publishers, 1941.

John Paul II. *Mulieris Dignitatem: Dignity and Vocation of Women*. Sherbrooke, PQ: Éditions Pauline, 1988.

———. *Redemptoris Mater: Mother of the Redeemer*. Sherbrooke, PQ: Éditions Pauline, 1987.

Lives of the Saints. Edited by Hugo H. Hoever, S.O.Cist. New York: Catholic Book Publishing Company, 1977.

Lumen Gentium: Dogmatic Constitution on the Church (Vatican II). In *The Documents of Vatican II*. Edited by Walter M. Abbott, S.J. New York: America Press, 1966.

National Liturgical Office. *Marian Year Prayers*. Ottawa, Ont.: Canadian Conference of Catholic Bishops, 1987.

Newman, John Henry. *Mary: The Second Eve*. Comp. Sr. Eileen Breen, F.M.A. In www.christendom-awake.org/pages/marian/newman1.

Order of Crowning an Image of the Blessed Virgin Mary. Washington, D.C.: U.S. Conference of Catholic Bishops, 1987.

Patron saints (index): In www.catholic-forum.com/saints.

Queen of Heaven. St. Paul, Minn.: Leaflet Missal Company, 1976.

Saint Joseph Daily Missal. Edited by Hugo H. Hoever, S.O.Cist. New York: Catholic Book Publishing Company, 1962.

Schineller, Peter, S.J. *Why We Honor Mary*. Liguori, Mo.: Liguori, 1989.

Weiser, Francis, X. *Handbook of Christian Feasts and Customs*. New York: Paulist Press, Deus Books, 1963.

Safe Travel; Our Lady of Salambao; Our Lady of Shongweni; Our Lady of Sorrows; Our Lady of Tears; Our Lady of Victory;

Subject Index